THE RULE OF GOD

BOOKS BY G. ERNEST WRIGHT

The Rule of God
Biblical Archaeology
The Biblical Doctrine of Man in Society
God Who Acts
The Old Testament Against Its Environment
The Challenge of Israel's Faith
The Westminster Historical Atlas to the Bible
(with Floyd V. Filson)
Ain Shems Excavations—(Parts IV and V)
(with Elihu Grant)
The Pottery of Palestine from the Earliest Times
to the End of the Early Bronze Age
The Book of the Acts of God (with Reginald H. Fuller)

THE
RULE
OF
GOD

ESSAYS IN BIBLICAL THEOLOGY

G. *George* ERNEST WRIGHT

(PARKMAN PROFESSOR OF DIVINITY,
HARVARD DIVINITY SCHOOL)

DOUBLEDAY & COMPANY, INC.
GARDEN CITY,
NEW YORK
1960

The quotation from Wisdom and Folly in Religion *by Joseph Haroutunian is reprinted by permission of the publishers, Charles Scribner's Sons.*

The quotations from the Revised Standard Version *of the Bible, copyrighted 1946 and 1952 by the Division of Christian Education, National Council of Churches, are reprinted by permission of the publishers, Thomas Nelson & Sons.*

PREFACE

The seven chapters of this book have been presented as lectures to various groups of Protestant clergymen and theological students during the last six years. In their present form they are the Carnahan Lectures at the Facultad Evangélica de Teología in Buenos Aires, Argentina, given June 2–5, 1959. Four of them were used as the Moore Lectures at the San Francisco Theological Seminary in 1954. Certain of them in various stages of their literary history have been given at McGill University, Western Theological Seminary in Holland, Michigan, Lutheran Theological Seminary in Maywood, Illinois, Dubuque Theological Seminary, Pittsburgh-Xenia Theological Seminary, McCormick Theological Seminary, the College of Preachers at the Washington (D.C.) Cathedral, the Synods of Ohio and New

England (United Presbyterian Church in the U.S.A.), and the New England Conference of Congregational and Christian Clergy. Earlier editions of Lectures I, III, and VI were published in the Canadian *Anglican Outlook and News Digest,* in successive issues of Vol. 9 (1953–54) between November and February. Much of the material in Lecture III is taken from the book by the writer and an ecumenical committee in Chicago, *The Biblical Doctrine of Man in Society* (London, Student Christian Movement Press, Ltd., 1954). In Parts I and II of Lecture VII, I have expanded certain insights of Professor H. Richard Niebuhr from an unpublished paper read by him to the Theological Discussion Group meeting in Washington, D.C., a few years ago. The inspiration for this address came from that brief paper.

Needless to say, I am deeply indebted to those who have invited me to lecture, and to those who have listened, for their courtesy and hospitality. Their encouragement has led me to present the lectures in published form in the hope that others may find them helpful.

Most of the Biblical citations are my own revision of the Authorized Version. Those from Isaiah 40–41 in Chapter I are quoted, as indicated, from the Revised Standard Version. The Index is a labor of love by my wife in the midst of her busy life as manager of our family.

JAFFREY CENTER, N.H.
JULY 14, 1959

G. ERNEST WRIGHT

CONTENTS

I

THE IDENTITY OF GOD:
AN EXPOSITION OF ISAIAH 40–41

There is something to be said for the ancient practice in polytheistic times of giving personal names to deities. Today we use the terms "divine," "deity," and "God," but none of them possess that particularity which a proper name affords. In any language name, essence and particularity are inextricably involved in one another. But when Judaism came to the position that the proper name "Yahweh" was too holy to pronounce, and when Christianity took over the Greek terms *kyrios* ("Lord") and *theos* ("God") for it, something was lost. "God" as a proper name is today used in many cultures and world views. Consequently, it conveys little until further defined. Even the early Church had difficulty with it, because it was a word used for the Stoic and Neo-Platonic deities as well as for the Deity

3

revealed in Jesus Christ. The general term is not necessarily particular, and it easily lends itself to confusion and syncretism.

In our time it has again become a virtue to say that one believes in "God"; indeed for many churches such a statement is virtually a sufficient qualification for entrance. Yet the basic and crucial question of the Church is, and must always be, not Church union, important as it may be, or the nature of the Church, important though that is, but rather: "Who is God?" How is he to be identified and known? And how is he to be served? To say "I believe" may mean little or nothing for my total existence. In whom do I believe? Do I say with Tillich that I believe in the object of "ultimate concern," and that when I am ultimately concerned I am a religious man? Is God the "the value creating process" of Whitehead? The "universe" of Schleiermacher, the "universal substance" of Spinoza, the "progressive integration" or "creative event" of Wieman, the "absolute spirit" of Hegel, or the indefinite and less absolute spirit invoked in our churches when we tritely and solemnly reiterate: "God is a spirit"?

One thing to be said about the Biblical God is this: he is known as the *Definite One*. He is no general and diffuse substance. He is not depicted as a general Idea, nor as a process. And he is not adequately described in "spiritual" terms. He sends the Spirit into human life, but he himself is too definite and dynamic a being to permit the categories of windiness and breathiness to be used of him. God as the Lord and Father of Jesus Christ is the absolute become particular and definite in the human scene, without in any way losing his infinity.

But to say that our God is the real One who stands revealed in Jesus Christ demands more explanation. Does the incarnation mean, for example, that we are now to worship Jesus Christ, while God himself recedes into the background, too absolute to be the focus of our religious attention, too gloriously enthroned to be approachable, too great to do anything in particular, and

4

hence too indefinite to command our absolute devotion? If so, what kind of a deity is Christ? Is he anything more than a beautiful Ideal who inspires us to be good and do good? Where, then, is the *active* Lord, the *coming* God?

I

In order to emphasize one all-important characteristic of the Lord and Father of Jesus Christ, I should like to turn briefly to chapters 40 and 41 of Isaiah. Chapter 40 begins with the call and commissioning of the prophet whom we call Second Isaiah. God in a heavenly assembly is heard commanding certain angelic messengers to go and comfort his people. We next hear one angel's voice make proclamation of the coming of the divine King: "Prepare the way of the Lord!" A second voice commands the prophet to cry out, and the prophet replies: "What shall I cry?" The received Hebrew text has here, "And he said" or "And one said." Yet the ancient versions, or Biblical translations, and the great scroll of Isaiah found in 1947 at Qumran by the Dead Sea, require us to vocalize the Hebrew as first person. The prophet is asking what God wants him to proclaim, "And *I* said, What shall I cry?" The answer of the angelic voice has to do, first, with the transitoriness of all things earthly in contrast to the enduring stability of God's Word. Therefore, the prophet is to arise as the herald of wonderful tidings. Judah is to behold its God who now comes to save, feeding the flock, gathering the lambs, and gently leading those with young. The promised day of salvation is at hand! Scattered and destroyed Israel is to be redeemed.

Second Isaiah stands at a great juncture of history; the Persian conqueror, Cyrus, is on the move, and the prophet is to proclaim what that means. It means the coming of the Lord! "Behold your God!"

Following this introduction, the prophet pauses throughout the remainder of chapter 40 to present a meditation for the broken people on the identity and nature of this God. He does so because there is no use of his proclamation unless faith and knowledge are restored. The clue to his problem is to be found in verse 27: "Why do you say, O Jacob, and speak, O Israel, 'My way is hid from the Lord, and my right is disregarded by my God'?" Who and what kind of a God is this one about whom we speak?

> Have you not known? Have you not heard?
> The Lord is the everlasting God,
>   the Creator of the ends of the earth.
> He does not faint or grow weary,
>   his understanding is unsearchable . . .
> Who has measured the waters in the hollow of his hand
>   and marked off the heavens with a span . . .
> Behold, the nations are like a drop from a bucket,
>   and are accounted as the dust on the scales; . . .
> To whom then will you liken God,
>   or what likeness compare with him?
> The idol! a workman casts it,
>   and a goldsmith overlays it with gold,
>   and casts for it silver chains.
> He who is impoverished chooses for an offering
>   wood that will not rot;
> He seeks out a skillful craftsman
>   to set up an image that will not move . . .
> To whom then will you compare me,
>   that I should be like him?
>   says the Holy One . . .
> He gives power to the faint,
>   and to him who has no might he increases strength.
>   (Isaiah 40:28, 12, 15, 18–20, 25, 29—R.S.V.)

The Identity of God

The God about whom the prophet speaks is the active Lord, known to be so because he is the Creator. He is Creator because he is Lord, and Lord because he is Creator. He is the *active* Sovereign now before whom the nations are as nothing. His power is the only power in the universe which is absolute. What he says, he will do. To what, then, in this visible universe is he to be compared? To the idols of men? Wooden things, however skillfully contrived, that will not move? Absurd! Well, then, the heavenly bodies whom the ancients worshiped? Yet not one of those bodies is missing because God by the greatness of his power has placed them where they are. There is nothing in creation to whom God can be compared, because what is is not the Maker, the thing ruled is not the Ruler. Yet this God is certainly known: the evidence of his ceaseless and powerful activity is all around us, in history and nature since the beginning. This, then, is the God who can renew your strength, make you run and not be weary, make you walk and not faint. Here is your God, and behold his return, his coming, is at hand!

In chapter 41 the prophet begins his prophecy, representing God as speaking directly through him. The thought turns immediately to the current historical scene. God is represented as issuing a summons to all the people of the earth to gather together in a great assembly: "let them approach, then let them speak; let us draw near for judgment." The subject to be discussed is the meaning of the Persian conqueror, Cyrus: "Who stirred up one from the east whom victory meets at every step . . . ? Who has performed and done this, calling the generations from the beginning? I, Yahweh, the first, and with the last; I am He." But the nations are represented as trembling with fright before Cyrus (as indeed they were)! So they are all industriously busy preparing their idols, encouraging each other, and saying of their handiwork: "It is good!"

7

Meanwhile God reminds Israel that she is his chosen. He has taken her from the ends of the earth. He has said: "You are my servant; I have chosen you and not cast you off . . . It is I who say to you, 'Fear not, I will help you.'" God has chosen Israel to the end "that men may see and know, may consider and understand together, that the hand of the Lord has done this, the Holy One of Israel has created it" (v. 20). Israel, God's specially created society, is, then, to be his witness in the current situation. She is the chosen, the servant, who is to affirm that "I am God, and even henceforth I am he; there is none that can deliver from my hand; I work and who can hinder it" (chap. 43: 10–13).

All now is in readiness for the council of the nations to begin. The people have their idols, and Yahweh his witness, Israel. Yahweh begins the proceedings by calling upon the gods of the nations to interpret what is going on, to explain past, present, and future, to do something either good or bad that they may be known to be gods.

> *Behold, you are nothing,*
> *and your work is nought;*
> *an abomination is he who chooses you.*
> *I stirred up one from the north, and he has come,*
> *from the rising of the sun, and he shall call on my*
> *name; . . .*
> *Who declared it from the beginning, that we might know,*
> *and beforetime, that we might say, "He is right"?*
> *There was none who declared it, none who proclaimed,*
> *none who heard your words.*
> *I first have declared it to Zion,*
> *and I give to Jerusalem a herald of good tidings.*
> *But when I look [at the gods] there is no one;*
> *among these there is no counselor*
> *who, when I ask, gives an answer.*

8

Behold, they are all a delusion;
their works are nothing;
their molten images are empty wind.

(Isaiah 41:24–29—R.S.V.)

The gods of mankind are here attacked at their weakest point. They were never conceived or devised as those whose primary function is a teleological control of history. They are known, first of all, by an image whom the worshiper sacramentally meets face to face, and outwardly by the activity of nature. Yet here is a God who affirms that he alone is God, that as Creator he is the active Lord of history, that historical events, when interpreted, reveal his work and the purpose in it, and that as the interpreter he has called into being, he has chosen as his servant, a special society. As Lord of history, he is Lord of time, the Creator of time, he who places meaning in past and present, and who provides a future. He is not one who is removed from history, and therefore to be known only by philosophical reason or mystical experience. He is the Absolute in the particular, and as such is the Definite One, the actively and concretely Real. Furthermore he is not allowing history to run a downward course until it reaches its abyss, its complete denouement, before he intercedes. He is the active One, the Coming One, he who creates the new thing (Isa. 43:19). He thus is our hope, for he creates hope, a hope that is in the now. And, having made history meaningful, he places vocation within it. He elects and he calls, and life achieves meaning in the vocation to which one is called.

II

Now, is such a god, identified in this way, the necessary *sine qua non,* the basic *a priori,* the one indispensable factor,

9

of the Christian faith? Can the meaning of Jesus Christ as God's climactic event in human history be comprehended if the Deity is described in any other way?

These, to me, are the crucial questions before the church of our day, because the tendency has been, implicitly where not explicitly, to answer in the negative. No, this is not the necessary identity of God for the Christian faith.

Why is it that the Biblical presentation of the active, definite, anthropomorphic Lord of history is no longer believed to be absolutely necessary for the Christian faith?

One reason among others that we may cite is that the Biblical view presupposes a radical difference between Creator and creation, wherein the Creator transcends, is independent of, exterior to, and outside of his creation. In depicting Biblical thought at this point it is almost impossible to avoid the use of spacial categories: "transcend," "be exterior to," or "outside of." The Biblical view of the universe is something confined and definite, to which God *can* be exterior. Today, however, we have what appears to be an infinite universe with limitless space. In fact, the universe is said to be expanding in the sense that the galaxies are thought to be moving away from one another, or from a center, at terrific speed. The mind simply cannot comprehend infinity, and, however limited or limitless space may turn out to be, it is all so vast and strange that it is simply impossible to see how the infinite Deity is exterior to or spacially transcends his seemingly infinite universe. Whatever God is, he simply cannot be depicted longer in spacial terms. If that is the case, how then can one ascribe definiteness, anthropomorphic activity, and personality to God? Definiteness and personality require a locus in space, or else they disappear. The human mind requires conceptions of form and space, so that it can say of the Real, here or there it is. What do these things mean? Who or what *is* God in such a universe?

To what can he be likened? We have a greater Unknown than did Second Isaiah. What, then, can and do we worship?

All of this is at the bottom of our modern skepticism and fuzziness about God. We have a universe in which there is no place for the Definite God, no place for heaven and none for hell. So the Definite He, the Lord and directing Sovereign of history, seemingly must give way. We are inclined to say that this is a mythology of the simple-minded past with no validity today. One of the central theological figures in Germany now is Rudolph Bultmann of Marburg, who has come out flatly and said that the cosmology of the Bible is no longer acceptable to the modern mind, and it simply must be demythologized. He has become a popular and controversial figure, not because all of his ideas are new, but largely because he is simply putting into words something we have all been feeling, but we have not given it such clear and explicit expression in a theological context.

In the churches there is still a great deal of bibliolatry which refuses to face the issue and simply evades or ignores it. But I would say that the dominant Protestant groups have long been aware of the problem, and have subtly tried to meet it. Biblical anthropomorphism has been suspect and avoided as far as possible; similarly heaven and hell, and, most important, history. Since God is no longer the real Sovereign and active Director of history in the Biblical sense, he must be conceived as real in a more diffuse and general way. The God of our churches has become more of an inner personal God, working within the inner resources of our souls or spirits. When we say anything about his being, we are inclined to use the categories of breath and wind which can be felt, but have no definite form or substance. God as the Definite Lord is set aside or merged with the Spirit, so that we believe we have said all that is necessary when we intone: "God is a Spirit." The following words, "and they that worship him must worship him in spirit and in truth," are not interpreted by the Biblical categories of thought, but more generally in terms of spiritual experience. A gentle kind of spiritual mysticism, to which are coupled the teachings of brotherly love and the immortality of our spiritual essence or soul, these have replaced the Biblical conceptions of radical obedience, corporate election, and historical vocation under the Lord of history. In Christ we are redeemed spiritually because he sets before us a beautiful example of a way of life, but the older objective explanations of the atonement no longer mean very much to us.

With such a God it is inevitable that we encounter difficulties in using the Bible. What do we mean, for example, when we recite the Lord's Prayer? "Hallowed be thy name." What does this mean, when *our* God does not require the category of holiness and when we live in a time when the whole concept of the holy is set aside? We know little of the mysterious holiness which produces real awe and reverence, and we have glimmerings of it only before a dead body. What do we mean when we pray, "Give us this day our daily bread"? In the Bible that makes sense, but our personal God of the spirit does not have as his primary function the active rulership of this universe. Man in a technological society produces his own bread in co-operation with the laws of nature. What we need to be delivered from are those catastrophes like war and depression which disrupt the technological organization of our society, an organization which insures us our food. Hence it should mean something for us to pray, "Deliver us from evil." Yet how does our personal God of the spirit do that? It is characteristic of him that he is fairly inactive as far as the world is concerned, and active only within us. He is not first of all the Lord of history; he is instead the diffuse object of our spiritual experience. He does not create historical hope within us. He comforts us and attempts to cleanse our spirits, but he is not the objective, Definite One who is in conflict with evil and will not rest or be defeated. He is not in triumphant control of history's crisis, and he does not say to us as he did to Second Isaiah: "I am God . . . ; there is none who can deliver from my hand; I work and who can hinder it."

Such would be my caricature of the God of our churches today, a God who has no objective reference, no dynamically active power, no holiness to produce reverence, no dangerous independence to produce fear and control obedience. All that is left in him is a diffusive spirit and love, with little power and no majesty.

III

Now, then, what do our philosophers and theologians do with the question of God today? Because of the need to find another locus, or place of standing, than historical revelation, one very popular tendency has been to seek God in the flux and movement of the world, either to identify him with it and thus to present an immanent God of the natural process not totally dissimilar in type from the head of a polytheistic pantheon—or to say with Greek philosophical idealism that God is the great idea or value or integration behind the world's process.

But one thing that the crises of our time have done is to reveal a demonic depth in the human personality and history. Philosophical idealism is not so easy today as it was in the age of Queen Victoria; it is becoming increasingly rare. Since the rediscovery of Kierkegaard, existentialism of one type or another has become far more popular among Christian thinkers. This is perhaps one of the most significant shifts in emphasis in our time. In existentialism we start, not with metaphysics or the universe and its process, but with the analysis of our human existence or situation, with its complex of relationships, with its frustrations, with its awareness of depth, possibility, and self-transcendence. By stressing the point that one cannot get behind the relationship of knower and the known, of subject and object, of the I and the other, the old dilemma of how the "I" knows anything is overcome. By stressing the awareness of depth and self-transcendence, a large realm of possibility in presenting the subject of God is opened up, if one feels the need to explore it.

There is much in this which is akin to the Biblical concentration on human existence. A new awareness of Biblical viewpoints has been opened which the last century's search for a process of evolving values could not discover. Nevertheless I am still not clear as to how one gets from self-analysis to the Biblical God, the Definite One whose revelation is historical. Rudolph Bultmann insists that the Bible must be demythed, that its world view must be interpreted as anthropological, not cosmological. But when he is finished, all he has left, seemingly, is the personal encounter with God which leads one to evaluate his existence in a new way. The God of history is gone, and only a God of personal encounter remains.

In my opinion, however, the most important figure in the Christian existentialist movement is Professor Paul Tillich. He is attempting to be a bridge in many directions. In theology he believes in the existence of the theological circle. One can begin at any point in that circle and soon reach every other point because all is tied in together. He chooses to begin, however, with the analysis of the self, with our being, because it is impossible for us to know anything about the being of the world except by analogy from the structure of our own beings. When one delves into the depth of the self, one finds there being which is individual, unique, unexchangeable, and yet which demands by its very nature participation because individuals share a common element, humanity. There are dynamics and form: that is, the drive, the power, the dynamic to be something, to become something, and also the actual form (i.e., the ministry or medicine or law) into which that drive has led. There are also freedom and destiny, the freedom of the struggle to choose and to reject in relation to my destiny, a destiny formed by nature, history, and myself.

Yet to be a self is also to be finite. To be something is to know a beginning and an end, to be faced with the possibility of "not to be," of non-being. To be human is constantly to be aware of finitude, of non-being. How does man have the courage to be, to live while trembling before the possibility of non-being? To be able to raise such a question means that the elements of man's being drive him to it, drive him to transcend himself. But if his ontology, or structure of being, forces him to transcend himself, how is he confined within the bounds of being? The answer is that he is not so confined. He belongs to the *ground* of being, to what is beyond the possibility of non-being, to being-itself to which one is bound and yet from which one is separated. Our trouble lies in the demonic which separates us from the ground of being, destroys unity, and brings tension. The drive always to be what one is not involves the demonic, though it also indicates that we have the possibility of knowing something more than tension, anxiety, non-being, but of knowing that we belong to the ground of being. We need not remain in this tension, for faith is possible, the knowledge of our belonging to being-itself, a faith based upon the New Being which is Christ. Christ as the New Being is not separated from the ground of being, and through him we can have the courage to be.

According to Tillich, all of the usual arguments for the existence of God are futile and prove nothing. The very phrase "existence of God" is contradictory because God does not "exist" in the way in which things or persons exist. "God becoming manifest under the conditions of existence," that is what happened in

Christ and is the Christological paradox. But God himself "does not exist. He is being-itself beyond essence and existence. Therefore, to argue that God exists is to deny him" (*Systematic Theology* I, 205).[1] Most of the so-called proofs of God seek to derive God from the given world. The "arguments move from special characteristics of the world to the existence of a highest being." This is just "as impossible logically, as it is impossible existentially to derive courage from anxiety" (p. 208). For example, the cause and effect chain leads the questioner back to a first cause. So God is the cause of everything. But the category "cause" belongs to the realm of being in opposition to, or polarity with, non-being: that is, cause and effect are a part of this finite world but God is no cause like other causes. Similarly, to say that God is transcendent is inadequate, because "transcendence" involves the idea of space, an above and a below. But space too belongs to the world, not to God. The same is true of the categories of time and substance. Space, substance, causality, and time cannot be ascribed to God. God is not substance or being threatened with non-being. He is not a being among other beings. He is the *ground* of being, the power of being, being-itself.

Tillich's abstract argumentation comes nearer than any other argument I know to what is implicit in Second Isaiah's question: "To whom then will you liken God?" There is nothing in this world of space and time which is like God. God is the ultimate mystery, the infinite depth, the ground, the power, and the source of all being.

The trouble with this type of reasoning, however, is that it comes nowhere near the Definite One, the Living God, the Coming Savior. These abstractions and the seemingly static

[1] *Systematic Theology* by Paul Tillich, 2 vols. (University of Chicago Press, 1951, 1957).

structure of thought with its three levels of being, ground of being, and demonic, can never in the world produce a living faith
or a living community of the faithful!

Tillich is aware of this problem, and he frankly says that a
doctrine of God cannot be derived from an ontological system.
"The character of the divine life is made manifest in revelation"
(p. 243). To be religious, he says, is to be ultimately concerned,
and one cannot be really concerned about abstractions like "the
ground of being." "The more concrete a thing is, the more
the possible concern about it. The completely concrete being,
the individual person, is the object of the most radical concern—
the concern of love" (p. 211). The absolute is abstract, but religious concern demands the definite and concrete. "This is the
inescapable tension in the idea of God," "the basic problem of
every doctrine of God" (p. 211). The gods of every religion, in-
cluding the Christian, generally fail us here because this tension
is too easily done away. God or the gods are thought to be beings,
"substances, caused and causing, active and passive, remember-
ing and anticipating, arising and disappearing in time and
space" (p. 212). Man is always trying to participate in them
and to use them for his own purposes. They are idols. And it
should be observed that in his way Tillich is as "death" to all
idolatry and man-made gods as is Second Isaiah. The Protestant
principle, from the prophets to our day, is a violent protest
against all religion itself which continually absolutizes the
relative.

Now, all that theology can say about God in non-symbolic
terms is that God is Being itself or the Absolute. Nothing else can
be said which is not symbolic. A symbol is an indirect statement,
not a direct one; it points beyond itself; it hints at reality without
confining it. "Religious symbols are double-edged. They are
directed toward the infinite which they symbolize *and* toward
the finite through which they symbolize it. . . . They open the

divine for the human and the human for the divine" (p. 240).
For many the term "symbol" carries the meaning of non-real,
and a number of movements have tried to interpret religious
language symbolically in order to dissolve the seriousness with
which that language is taken. But in classical usage this is not
the case. Symbols "give to God and to all his relations to man
more reality and power than a non-symbolic . . . interpretation
could give them" (p. 241). They are proper and necessary, and
theology can only interpret them, not negate them.

The Biblical God, to Tillich, is one who is presented, and who
presents himself to us, in symbolic terms. He is the concrete
God, the Lord who led Israel from Egypt and the Father of
Jesus Christ. He is individual, personal, definite, but all this without being an idol. He is independent of his nation, Israel, and of
his own individual nature as known by the symbols. "If the nation breaks the covenant, he still remains in power. He proves
his universality by destroying his nation in the name of principles which are valid for all nations—the principles of justice.
This undercuts the basis of polytheism. It breaks through the
demonic implications of the idea of God, and it is the critical
guardian which protects the holy against the temptation of the
bearers of the holy to claim absoluteness for themselves. The
Protestant principle is . . . an attack against a self-absolutizing
and, consequently, demonically distorted church" (p. 227).

I suspect that there is a great deal that we could say in
criticism of Tillich: e.g., the static nature, as it seems, of his
structure of being, or of being-itself and the ground of being.
Central to Biblical thought is the category of activity and movement by which the Absolute is known. We might also remind
ourselves of the current notion of modern physics, derived from
Einstein, that matter is motion by and large. Who knows, perhaps activity and being are one in some way. Yet the value of
Tillich, as I see the matter, is that he is facing squarely the

18

problem of modern doubt with regard to God. He is resurrecting in believable form the whole study of ontology, which in other forms used to be called metaphysics. He is attacking our intellectual problem in our modern world.

But even more interesting to me is Tillich's virtual admission that, by means of such an approach, or by any approach, one cannot get to the Biblical Lord of history, the Definite One, who alone can produce faith and obedience. This God is known only by revelation, and he is depicted only by symbolic language. Tillich by attacking modern doubt clears the mind for the reception of these symbols and shows to a limited extent what they do not mean, while hinting at what they mean.

A crucial question before us in the Church has to do with the nature and adequacy of our symbols. To whom or to what will ye liken God? The symbol of the Living God, the active Lord, the Definite One, the Sovereign of history and community, this has been so weakened that we have sought substitutes for it. But these substitutes cannot sustain the Church. Nor can they produce a living, obedient faith, able to overcome the division of sacred and secular, triumph and disaster, history and religious experience, vocation and devotion. In this God alone can the Church move through history with its vocation, without being weary, walking without fainting.

The apostle Paul in his first Corinthian letter contrasts the wisdom of the world, the wisdom of God, and the language in which the two are expressed. He wrote: "Now we have received, not the spirit of the world, but the spirit which is from God, that we might understand the gifts bestowed on us by God. *And we impart this in words, not taught by human wisdom, but taught by the Spirit, interpreting spiritual truths in spiritual language*" (I Cor. 2:12–13, R.S.V. Margin; italics mine).

2

THE NATURE OF MAN:
AN EXPOSITION OF GENESIS 3

One of the crucial passages of Scripture in the history of Christian exegesis is the third chapter of Genesis. I venture to say that, because of what this chapter tells us about man, Christianity and Judaism possess a doctrine of man that differentiates them from other religions. Furthermore, this chapter constantly acts as a corrective to those in both faiths who would adopt more idealistic conceptions. An exegetical study of this chapter is perennially fruitful.

1. First, let us ask the question as to the authorship and date of the Adam and Eve stories in chapters 2–4 of the Book of Genesis. Fortunately, this is not a difficult question to answer. Nearly all critical scholars today are agreed about the author-

ship, and they do not diverge very widely in the matter of date. These chapters are considered to be a part of the J or Yahwist document. While many scholars of the previous generation dated this work to about the time of the prophet Elijah, that is, about 850 B.C., I suspect that a majority of the scholars of this generation would say without too much hesitation that it was the product of the court of David, or, more probably, of Solomon, in the tenth century B.C. But how should this document be conceived? Here again, we may say that modern scholarship is fairly well agreed on the supposition that the Yahwist was a collector of the early traditions of Israel, who edited and put them together in such a way that they would form a proper confessional epic for the nation of Israel, newly re-created in strength by King David. It is a remarkable piece of work, the earliest extensive collection of historiographical materials known from the ancient world. On the other hand, we understand that the unknown author of this epic was not writing simply for personal pleasure. He was collecting and interpreting the traditional materials in such a way that they would adequately confess the nation's faith. Here was a people who could only explain what they were by telling the story of their past in terms of the mighty work of God. To tell the story was thus to confess the faith and to give praise to Israel's divine Lord.

The Yahwist document is the first written edition of this classic story of which we know, and it forms the basis of our present Hexateuch. It can be traced with considerable certainty in the books of Genesis, Exodus, and Numbers. After that, however, scholars are not at all sure as to its identity, and there is little agreement. The prehistoric traditions that were taught to Israel in Genesis 1–11 are basically those first presented in the court of Solomon by our historian. Subsequently, during the sixth or fifth century, the Jerusalem priesthood in exile in Babylon edited this old material by adding a new introduction in chapter 1–2:

4a, by providing a genealogical framework in chapters 5–11 and by elaborating the older material by supplementation, particularly in the matter of the Flood story and the covenant with Noah. As far as can now be seen, however, the original purpose and intent of the Yahwist writer in chapters 2–4 was not changed by this later editing and supplementation.

2. Second, we must ask the question as to the form, or type, of literature contained within our chapter. It would appear to be a very individual type of material that is unlike anything else that is in the Bible. At first glance, it would appear to be one segment of a people's traditional history of the world and of human origins, such as was taught by one generation to another. Yet a closer look at the material suggests that it is not given as a series of obvious facts to be accepted or rejected as fact. It possesses a deeper dimension. To be sure, in the Bible as a whole, fact and event, history interpreted by faith, have a very close and inseparable relation. Yet here the didactic intent, or parabolic aim, is so obvious that for a parallel one might turn to the parables of Jesus. Yet the difference is also apparent, when we recall that this traditional story of human origins is not a fable or narrative made up to serve a particular teaching occasion. That is to say, the tenth-century writer was scarcely conscious of the problem of fact and faith in the way that we are today. *We* are very conscious of this problem, and we want to ask continually whether or not something really happened as a tradition says that it did. This very self-conscious type of inquiry is what separates us from our writer and those he taught. Even so, however, our center of interest must be at the point where his was. That is to say, we must primarily be interested in his question, not in ours, if we would exegete the passage. *Our* first question is: Did it happen? He is uninterested in such a question, perhaps because this is something which everyone amongst his people more

or less took for granted. In telling the story, however, his question has to do with the problem of man as man; it is not primarily concerned with a factual history of creation. His problem has to do with the profound question as to why a creature of the wondrous God finds himself within history in such a miserable state.

In other words, an analysis of the literary form of the chapter suggests that we do not have in Genesis 3 a story, the central purpose of which is merely to present a history of man, but a traditional narrative which is employed to interpret the life of man in history—not so much the history of the origin of sin, as an interpretation of the fact of sin.

3. In the third place, what can be said about the traditional material behind this story? The author is surely not creating something out of nothing; he is using pre-existent material, though the exact form and history of his traditions are unknown. Central to the story, however, are the following: (a) the Garden of Eden, which is the primordial paradise; (b) the first man, who does not bear a proper name. The Hebrew word *Adam* was never used by the Israelites as a word suitable for a personal name. In this chapter *Adam* means "the man" in the most general sense. The fact that the term is used at all indicates that primordial man is considered in a generic aspect, that is, his name is mankind; (c) then there are the two trees in the Garden, the tree of life and the tree of the knowledge of good and evil, symbolic names obviously borne by no species of historical tree!

We know that ancient Babylonia also had a traditional picture of a paradise in primordial times. Furthermore, we know that western Asia had a great interest in the tree of life. This tree seems to appear very frequently in ancient art; it surely played a very much larger role in everyday life and thought than the mythological texts that have survived would indicate.

The Nature of Man

One of the central concerns of man in Biblical times was the problem of life, life in which there was no death. Death was the horror from which an escape was sought. The multitudinous forms of weakness, sickness, trouble, anything which circumscribed the freedom and joy of one's activity—these could be interpreted as a manifestation that death was in the midst of life. Life without death, therefore, was an important speculation to ancient man. In Egypt the meaningful reality of death was actually denied. The end of this mortal existence was but the transition point from life on earth to life in fellowship with the gods, from humanity to divinity. The king was an incarnate god, and in the blessings enjoyed by him his people would likewise share.

In western Asia, however, life was much more difficult and fragile. Death was a grimmer and more problematical reality. One of the most interesting of the classic tales of western Asia was the Babylonian epic of Gilgamesh. This is the story of a man's search for life, and of his failure to find it. He was a king of a city in southern Babylonia, a great hero and a mighty man of valor. So active and energetic was he that his people besought the gods that some outlet for his energies be provided and that they be delivered from his constant ministration! A great companion was provided him by the gods, and the two of them together performed mighty exploits until the friend killed the bull of heaven and for this himself was put to death by the gods. Gilgamesh now was inconsolable. Hitherto, his only thought of death was the glorious death of a hero, killed in some marvelous deed of valor. Now, however, his friend was gone, torn from him, leaving him without hope and with no way whereby this personal tie could be mended. Disregarding the advice of his people, he set out on a long search for life. He finally arrived at the River of Death, and the boatman ferried him across it. There in what was evidently the primordial paradise he found the Baby-

lonian Noah, the one man in the history of the human race who
had been granted immortality by the gods. To him Gilgamesh
appealed for aid, but this appeal was without effect. The Babylonian immortal can only tell the story of the almost accidental
circumstances in which he had received life. These circumstances involve the Babylonian story of the primordial flood.
Enlil, the king of the gods and the personification of the storm,
found man a most troublesome creature after his creation. The
god's sleep was disturbed, and, in a fit of rage, he decreed a
flood which would put an end to all mankind. The flood in the
Babylonian account, therefore, is within the context of the
search for life—a very different context than that given in the
Bible. Furthermore, in Babylon in contrast to Israel the flood
is a rash and irresponsible act of a god in anger. To counteract
and to balance this rash act, the flood hero is told by another
of the gods to build the ark and to save himself, his family,
and two of every type of creature. As a reward for his deeds
he is granted eternal life without death. Hence, he con-
cludes his sorrowful tale to Gilgamesh by saying that what
has happened to him can happen never again; his blessing
cannot be transferred to all mankind. As Gilgamesh turns
to leave, however, the flood hero's wife tells him of a certain
plant at the bottom of the River of Death which, when eaten,
has the power of rejuvenation. On his return, Gilgamesh found
this plant and started across the desert with it, back to his own
city. After a hot day, he encountered an oasis, stripped off his
clothes for a bath. While he was thus refreshing himself, however, a serpent smelled the plant, darted from its hole, and took
it away. Thus it comes about, the ancient Babylonian believed,
that snakes never die—they merely shuffle off their skin—but man
must die! On this bitter, and rebellious, note the great epic ends.

In the Bible, by contrast, we note, however, that the tree of life
is no longer the central theme. At one stage in the history of the
tradition it may well have played a larger role than it does in the

final edition preserved for us in the canonical scriptures. But, for our unknown tenth-century theologian, it is a simple fact of existence which must be accepted without question that the tree of life is denied man. Man is mortal, death is his lot, to dust he shall return. Why is this the case? How did it come about that the wondrous goodness of God should have so decreed in the creation? It is this searching "why" which is our writer's central concern.

4. In the fourth place, we must look more closely at the second tree, the tree of the knowledge of good and evil. As far as we now know, there was no such tree amongst the mythologies of the neighboring peoples. Yet the story in the third chapter of Genesis shows certain indications of having had a background and history before it has reached its present form. The talking snake was certainly once a mythological element. In its present form, however, the snake is demythologized; it is not a god or goddess of wisdom; it is only a beast of the field which the Lord God has made. Its mythological background survives only in the function it performs and in the fact that it is allowed to speak. We note a similar ancient background for the snake in Jesus' reference when he says that his followers should be "wise as serpents and harmless as doves." There is no reason why a snake should be particularly wise, unless one recalls the long mythological history behind the poor creature.

Furthermore, a pagan, or at least a very early, background of the story may be suggested in the sexual consciousness that still survives. At one stage, the Genesis 3 account may also have been a part of the ancient mythological search for life. To know good and evil, therefore, in its original context may have referred to the mysterious principle of fertility and reproduction in which the life of man shares the life of the gods which is the life of nature in polytheistic thought.

All this, however, is far in the background of the present

narrative and can only be conjectured. The peculiar and distinctive part of the story as we have it now is that the whole focus of attention is upon the tree of the knowledge of good and evil; it is not upon the tree of life. We are not told precisely what is meant by the tree of knowledge; its meaning is only suggested, not defined. Whatever it precisely designated or was intended to designate, it immediately focuses attention upon the will of man rebelling against his Creator. This is a most unusual note, a most remarkable portrayal in either an ancient or a modern setting—a free man using his will power against his Creator and Lord. This is seen as the human problem; this is the center of the story. The knowledge man gets from his eating of the forbidden fruit is a knowledge which enables him to use the goodness of God's creation to evil ends. The central problem of human existence, then, does not lie in nature; it lies within the human will. Man's central concern, therefore, should not be eternal life —that is God's gift or prerogative—but with the relation of his will to the will of God.

5. From the story we note the fact of man's freedom, and the fact that free will is power which can be used against a divine command.

In one sense this is the source of the Biblical conception of the dignity of man. Human dignity does not lie in a divine nature, or even in an unlimited capacity for creativity. Man's dignity rests in the fact that he has been addressed by God; he is the recipient of the divine command. He alone amongst all the creatures of earth has an "ought" or a "must" addressed to him. But he has used his free will to rebel. Responsibility and freedom of decision in relation to that responsibility—this is surely what the Jerusalem priest who is responsible for giving to us the first chapter of Genesis must have meant by the phrase "the image of God." In these two terms, responsibility and freedom, what is meant by the similarity to the divine in man exists. But, we might say, for man freedom lies in the mystery of his creation by God, while responsibility lies in his election, his calling to labor as God's servant.

6. Furthermore, in the sixth place, the story implies a judgment on man. He rebels. His dignity, the office of kingship over the whole creation in which he has been installed by God, this is not the real point of the story for the Yahwist writer. The real question is: Why has he rebelled? Why has this noble creature refused his creaturehood? The Biblical understanding of man actually centers at this point: he is one who has betrayed his creaturehood. His power has become a lust for self-divinization. It is not that the power given him is an evil in itself; but it has surely been used to an evil end.

Man the rebel, man the sinner—this is scarcely a self-evident proposition. This is not the first thing that occurs to the normal human being when he seeks to describe himself and the lot of his kind. It is an insight, achieved only within the Biblical doctrines of election and covenant, only in the story of a people who have been addressed by God, and given their mission by God, but nevertheless whose history is a history of betrayal of covenant and disobedience to the goodness of God.

7. In the seventh place, man's sin has brought the divine judgment. Nature, of course, is far from the perfect creation it was meant to be. Why? Not because of an incomplete evolution, but because of judgment. The whole understanding of the world revolves around the judgment. Nature is under a curse for man's sake. Indeed, the story of civilization on earth also is to be seen as hanging from the fact of sin. By the very juxtaposition of traditional stories, our author presents his view of the progress of civilization. In chapter 4 the separation of nomadic and

agricultural pursuits is accompanied by the first murder. The building of the first city is accompanied by the story of Lamech, whose life is a life of vengeance, a vengeance that elsewhere in scripture is something belonging to God alone and not to man. Lamech is the picture of man's ultimate degradation in a life apart from God. At the close of the Flood story (chapter 8), we are told about the introduction of vineyard culture, one of the basic industries of the Palestinian and Syrian areas. And this is accompanied by the picture of the good man, Noah, drunk! The distribution and blessing of the nations in chapter 10 is accompanied by the Tower of Babel story. In the latter mankind thrusts its creation into heaven itself, saying: "Let us get us a name!" Civilization at each stage is accompanied by its spiritual problems, and the meaning of the whole is that it knows nothing whatsoever of its responsibility to its sovereign Creator.

Evil in this early material is both an act of man's will and a state in which he lives. Man wills to sin and this also creates a state of sin, both as an aspect of man's willed act and as the judgment of God. Indeed, the Hebrew word for evil (ra) means both things. It can refer to an ethical decision, a willed act; but it can refer at the same time to the concomitant psychical, social, and material results or penalties. In this way the word can mean a sinful act of the will or it can mean the state of society in which we live, or even the suffering or harm that may come at any one moment in any situation. Hence, man sins, and he lives in a state of sin. He wills to sin and he is born into sin. Recall the well-known words in the Fifty-first Psalm: "Against thee and thee only have I sinned." This is the willed act. Yet these words are followed in the psalm by the following: "Behold I was brought forth in iniquity and in sin did my mother conceive me." This is not a direct reference to a willed act on the part of the mother, but to the sinful society in which we live. Recall the words of the prophet Isaiah who, after the vision of the holiness of God, confesses that he is an unclean man in the midst of an unclean people.

One of Israel's most ancient and marvelous confessions of faith is preserved in Exodus 34 (vv. 6–7). Here God, in revealing his name to Moses, expounds the meaning of the name through the quotation of the old liturgical confession. This confession speaks of the marvelous love and patience of God in his dealings with his people, but it adds that, while God keeps his lovingkindness for thousands, forgiving iniquity and transgression and sin, "he will by no means acquit the guilty, visiting the iniquity of the fathers upon the children, and upon the children's children, unto the third, even the fourth generation." This is an empirical description of the fact of evil and suffering in the world, that the deeds of the father do cause consequences which are felt by the generations of the children. Such is the state in which we live in history.

The doctrine, so important in Christian theology, of human depravity, or of original sin, means just this. We are born into and live in a state of sinfulness. Cain, Lamech, the nations—they all possess an inner infection; there is no real soundness in them; there is a state of sinfulness, though specific acts of the responsible will continue.

How has this situation in human affairs come about? The tenth-century Yahwist writer can only tell a story, an old story about a tree of the knowledge of good and evil. Man (mankind) ate the forbidden fruit of all knowledge, a knowledge that gave him power for evil, an evil to which even the good can be used. Man has used his freedom and his power to attempt to acquire a divine knowledge, to become a god or a divine being in his own right; this is his denial of his creaturehood. This is the source of his woe.

A few years ago, Professor Richard Niebuhr of Yale University, in unpublished remarks at a meeting of the Theological Discussion Group in Washington, D.C., said that in his opinion there are two common ways of understanding man which are current amongst us. One is through the myth of the fall of Adam. The other is through the myth of *Pithecanthropus erectus*. The one is tenth century B.C. within the third chapter of Genesis. The other has to do with our ancestry, the long evolution of the human being, beginning within and perhaps before the Pleistocene age of geologic history. Which of the two is true?

Another way of putting the matter, Professor Niebuhr continued, is to think of man in terms of the vast ruin of the Colosseum in Rome. It is a spectacular, awe-inspiring building. Though it is in ruins, still it is awesome and one must respect it. Another way is to think of man in terms of a modern ranch house of the type being built by the thousands upon thousands around the edges of our cities. The ranch house can be an attractive, neat, and extremely comfortable small home. Furthermore, it has the capacity for great expansion. One wing can be added after another. Dreams and great possibilities go hand in hand in its construction. No one knows where it has to end!

Which of these two pictures presents a truer understanding of man? Which picture presents the greatest appreciation of the dignity of man? The Colosseum is a noble and tremendous structure even in its tattered state. The ranch house is attractive, small but perhaps adequate, convenient, and possessing great potential. In some sense, perhaps, both are true. Yet it perhaps must be remembered that modern totalitarianisms have grown, not out of the Colosseum, but out of the ranch house! Not out of the myth of Adam, but out of disillusion with *Pithecanthropus erectus!* Disillusionment cannot affect the ruined Colosseum; it perhaps may give one a more realistic appreciation of it. But the hopes and dreams behind the ranch house can quickly perish. And housing authorities are beginning to wonder whether or not our vast new suburbs may not be the slums of tomorrow.

3

INDIVIDUAL AND COMMUNITY:
THE BIBLICAL DOCTRINE OF SOCIETY

It was just over a century ago, on July 8, 1853, that Commodore Perry with four ships dropped anchor off Japan and opened its feudal gates to the invasion of Western civilizaton. For the past one hundred years the East has been receiving a stream of Westerners; and a stream of ironical events has occurred. On the one hand, trade has flourished; on the other, idealists have seen the opportunity of extending freedom, democracy, and Christianity. Ancient social and political structures of the East have collapsed, but the ideals of the West have not necessarily been followed. As a former colleague, Dr. Theodore F. Romig, has pointed out: "the triumph of the West has resulted in new forms of totalitarianism, not democracy;

nationalism, not patriotism; communism, not faith in God."[1]
"When West touches East," he continues, "must there always
follow convulsions and the emergence of violent demonic forces?
Must our enlightenment turn into darkness, our democracy into
slavery, and the Christian hope into an earthly Utopianism
which ends in bloodshed and disillusionment? What is wrong?"
Korea—the most Christianized nation of the East, recently a
battlefield of the world! China, America's friend, now enemy,
turning Communist while ruled by a Christian leader and while
Dr. J. Leighton Stuart, a Christian, scholar, and popular friend
of the Chinese, was our U.S. ambassador. Kenya, perhaps the
best governed territory in Africa with a Christian Church that is
comparatively strong, and yet the scene of the bloody Mau Mau
terror!

I am told that we must not interpret the Mau Mau and other
similar African movements as simply the mad outburst of de-
praved primitives. Their leaders are educated men who blame
the white man for everything wrong. But what have we done?
Have we not brought good government, an end to tribal warfare,
modern sanitation and medicine, welfare agencies, schools, the
machine, and everything good?

Yes, but in doing it we have done something else. We have
shaken the foundations of native life and deprived the tribe of
its very reason for existence. A Kikuyu man, working in a
town, separated from land and clan, having to cope with the
powerful white man, is a lonely and completely lost soul. We
have broken his tribe and put nothing in its place but welfare
agencies. The white man with generally good intentions destroys what to folk society is the very lifeblood of its existence
without creating anything to replace it. The people of Asia are

[1] "When Shall the Twain Meet?" *McCormick Speaking*, May, 1953,
p. 7.

substituting nation, race, or party for ancient social structures, such as the caste and family systems of India and China. As Dr. Romig has put it, "Nationalism, Shintoism and Communism are sophisticated expressions of Mau Mauism, all of which seek to rebuild" from the ruins of broken tribal and folk society. In Alan Paton's book, *Cry the Beloved Country*, two African ministers are conversing. One says to the other: "You cannot stop the world from going on. The tragedy is not that things are broken, but that they are not mended again. . . . It suited the white man to break the tribe, but it has not suited him to build something in the place of what is broken. . . . They are not all so. There are some white men who give their lives to build up what is broken—but they are not enough."

I

One of the central problems of our time is the problem of man and society, and we Christians are in something of a dilemma because we do not know the answer any better than anyone else. We do not know how to separate our Christianity from our culture. To be a missionary is to be also in some measure a cultural ambassador of the West. But what kind of a religion do we export? Is it an individualistic piety which has been tailored to fit a democracy in which individual freedom of life and expression is proclaimed as the highest good?

With single-minded intensity we Westerners have clung since the Renaissance to a humanistic view of man the individual, with the result that the sense of the meaning of community has been evaporating. Society has been atomized; but individual freedom has not answered the social problem. In the industrial economy of our time we now hear of "mass man." The free individual has become lost in the mass we are told, and his lostness involves his loss of community. A chaotic emptiness endangers us, stablized on the one hand by great industrial power and a frantic search for the meaning of our democratic tradition, and on the other by totalitarian movements which view man the individual as simply a segment of "mass man," who for his own good must be directed or pushed toward a goal determined by the state or elite party within it.

Even the churches have so reflected our modern preoccupation with individual man that, no matter how high the doctrine of the Church to which a particular confession may ideally adhere, whether Presbyterian, Episcopal, or what, all are actually in the same boat. In practice our congregations are a gathering of individuals, motivated by a desire to be decent citizens in possession of peace of mind, but knowing little of Christian community in the Biblical sense and expecting little from it. The Church's theology, so vigorously theocentric, is now dominated by anthropology. The Church's worship is largely concerned, not with social organism, but with the individual's need of peace, rest, and joy in the midst of the storms and billows of life. Our so-called "gospel" hymns are not necessarily objective, but inclined to be self-centered: "Will there be any stars in *my* crown?"; "Blessed assurance, Jesus is *mine!*" The real subject of attention is the big "I," and we may contrast such great theocentric and confessional hymns as "A mighty fortress is our God," and "O God, our help in ages past, our hope for years to come." The sectarianism of the churches, their racial and national cleavages, are further expression of an individualism which distorts the nature of Christian society and provides excuse for the world's individualism.

II

Small wonder, then, that the modern Christian is inclined to study the Bible in a manner not unlike the pagan's study of his sacred literature, the purpose being to find inspirational, devotional, and moral enlightenment for personal living, and nothing more. In sophisticated and scholarly circles, beginning in the last century, the tendency has been to make the Bible speak in support of our individualism. What is the Bible? One answer has been that it is the story of a people's discovery of ideals and values. Among these values is the emergence of the individual as a responsible being. In the early days of Israel the individual was lost, dominated, submerged by the tribal mass. That is the reason the nation is the focus of attention. Gradually, however, this tribal ethic broke down and the individual was liberated. Two different New Testament scholars within the last fifteen years have written that it was Jesus who first "discovered the individual"—surely a statement so poorly informed that it is actual nonsense! Most scholars have said that individual responsibility first appeared with Jeremiah and Ezekiel. One has written, for example: "Jeremiah from his own experience knew that the essence of religion was personal relationship between God and the individual."[2]

But did Jeremiah know any such thing? Most improbable! So convinced have we been that the true nature of religion consists in a dialogue between God and individual man that we have been quite willing to force the Bible to say what we want it to say. After all, however, we now know that by the time Israel

[2] B. M. Pickering in Gore, Goudge and Guillaume, eds., *A New Commentary on Holy Scripture* (New York, 1928), p. 488.

41

appears on the scene of history primitive man with his weakly developed consciousness of himself as a responsible "I" had largely disappeared from the scene of history. The primitive conceptions of collective guilt may still be seen occasionally, but only as traces or relics from the distant past. In all ancient codes of law the individual is a responsible person, subject to penalty in a court of law. It is no surprise to discover, therefore, that in Israel's earliest laws collective retribution as a legal penalty does not exist. To be sure, we read stories of isolated cases where social solidarity in the assignment of guilt still existed, as in the slaying of the sons of Saul (II Sam. 21). But such actions were outside the law. The latter did everything it could to control them. Each person was a subject at law and morally responsible for his actions.

III

Furthermore, in Israel this personal responsibility was given focus in the Lawgiver, God. Obedience was supposed to arise, not from legal necessity, but from complete commitment to the Lord who had brought the people into existence. God out of grace had given to this people, who formerly had not known the protection of law, a revealed order by which they could live. In the law of this order God's characteristic address to his people was in the form, "Thou Shalt." This type of personal command could only appear in a particular covenant relationship wherein God was known as the one personal Lord to whom alone belong all rights of sovereignty. This religious grounding of law promptly invaded the neutral law of civil community with the result that legal violation was more than civil violation; it was violation of commitment to the community's Lord. Hence a sense of sin existed, unknown elsewhere in this sense, which brought into focus the ideas of betrayal and rebellion. There also existed a sense of joy and exaltation in obedience, in the doing of God's will—something without precedent, because for most people then and now religious exaltation appears elsewhere than in service and vocation.

God's law gave the revealed order to the community; but the law was by no means a tribal ethic. It transcended the limitations of such primitivism and formed the basis of a *new society,* which in both popular and prophetic eschatology was seen as the first fruits of God's universal Kingdom. Yet the individual was not lost or submerged in this community order. In that order God's "Thou Shalt" was characteristically singular. God's word singled out each person, so that as a responsible "I" the individual heard the Word addressed to him personally. In the covenant with the nation God dignified each member or citizen with his personal address. The Lord of the nation was the Lord of each of its individuals.

Now when the Church in its study of the New Testament comprehends this situation in Israel as the divine preparation for the Body of Christ, it will be better prepared to comprehend the meaning of Christ's "individualism." Far from first "discovering the individual," the work of Christ was actually for the purpose of clearing the way of entrance into the *new* community, ordained of old and ardently awaited. The Sermon on the Mount is firmly rooted in the legal tradition of Israel. Its prescriptions, like God's "Thou Shalt" of old, were chiefly addressed to the individual. Yet attention is focused, not on the individual in and for himself, but on the manner of the Kingdom, for the time was at hand and individual decision and commitment were required. Man as man finds himself confronted with a choice, but awaiting him is the new community, the first fruits of that which shall be. In other words, the relationship of individual and community in the New Testament is in *essential* aspects precisely that which existed in Israel.

We may thus maintain that we possess in the Bible, not a description of the development of true individualism after the pattern of modern humanism, but instead the portrayal of the true relationship between man and community in which the nature of both is revealed. Furthermore, the Bible also reveals the nature of our chief problem: Life under the divine call and revelation in a world for which we are responsible, a world whose principalities and powers continually threaten to overwhelm us. We are threatened, not alone by outward attack, but especially by the more subtle interior and silent working, which ends in blinding our eyes and weakening our commitment.

So, we ask again: What is the Bible? The answer must be something like this: *The Bible is primarily a confessional history in which the acts of God are interpreted as bringing into being a new society, a society which is the divine answer to the alienation and degradation of the people of the world.* No wonder, then, that the Bible gives its primary attention to a people, to Israel and the Church rather than to individuals as such. To us and to most of the world's religions the central issue ought to be the life of the individual in his world. Not so in the Bible! There the real concern is with the community in which each individual is called to participate. The formation of the community is God's central act of grace; to it he has revealed its election, its task, its goal. But what of the individual? Does not anyone pay attention to him? Surely, but his greatest need is to be delivered from his big "I," from self-centeredness, self-idolatry. Consequently, he finds his true life when he possesses a calling within the community, when his election is understood to fulfill a portion of the community election, when, in complete loyalty to the Lord, who binds all diversity into unity, he discovers the time of his life to be overarched by the time of the new community, which in turn is transcended by the redemptive purpose of God. Man the individual is called to obedient service, not in order that he himself can be God, but that he may find his true being in participation, in doing what his God-given vocation calls him to do.

IV

Involved in this viewpoint is the conception of man as a social being by his very created structure. He is man only in the midst and as a member of a people; he was created for society. It is not good for him to be alone: so the creation story in Genesis 2 affirms. With such a view it is impossible for the Bible to think of individual man as existing in and for himself. It is equally difficult for the Bible to think in terms of an abstract universalism in which the individual's relation to God rather than the problem of society is the focus of attention.

Yet we must note certain things about this Biblical community:

1. It was not believed to be a natural formation; it was instead thought to be a special divine creation. To Israel and to the Church the central form of confession was historical, testifying to what God had done in redeeming and establishing his people. Worship and the sacraments were likewise centered in historical memory and commemoration, for God had chosen and redeemed his people, separating them out from the peoples of this world. Worship united past and present generations in the acts of God which had created the new society.

2. It is characteristic of this new community to think of itself and to speak of itself as a people rather than as an organization. It was a new people of God, not a club, a sect, or first of all a political order among other kingdoms of the earth. The factors of race, blood, and genealogy would never in themselves have

45

created Israel as we meet her on the pages of the Old Testament. Here in ideal was a people of God, and such a conception always stood in tension with actual Israel as a nationalistic order.

In the New Testament the vocabulary used of the new community clearly suggests the conception of organism, rather than organization: "the family of Christ," "the household of faith," "the New Covenant," "assembly," "synagogue," "fellowship," "body of Christ," "bride of Christ," a vine with its branches, etc. The true meaning of *ecclesia* (church) is to be discovered, not by Greek etymology, but by examination of the meaning of these terms. Several of them indicate the special relationship existing between the people and Christ, which reveals the inner basis of community life. For example, the Johannine figure of the vine (John 15): Christ the Vine, the individuals as the branches. Or the Pauline figure of the Body of Christ. "Body" here in its Biblical sense is not a structure in which the mind or spirit or soul is imprisoned, but the total person as a living organism. Hence the body of Christ is Christ himself. To speak of the community as Christ's body is to emphasize the fact that it is a living, unified organism by means of the principle of corporate personality so common in the Semitic world. Christ is the community and the community is "in Christ." This manner of speaking is anticipated in the Gospels, where the disciples are identified with Christ: e.g., "he who received you receives me" (Matt. 10:40). Individual members with their variety of talents can be likened to the members of the body, so that "there are many parts, yet one body" (I Cor. 12:20). In the life of the body Christ can be conceived as the head, "from whom the whole body, nourished and knit together through its joints and ligaments, grows with a growth that is from God" (Col. 2:19).

Other New Testament figures, such as "the family of Christ," "the household of faith," the "fellowship," all point to the same conception: namely, that the new community is a people knit together, not primarily by human structures of organization, but instead by an inner mutuality of spirit provided by God in Christ. Behind such terms lies the Old Testament conception of a people bound in a living covenant with its Lord. Community in the Bible is a psychic harmony of individual souls, held together by mutual vows in covenant with the Lord and sharing the common blessing which he confers. The harmony of will is not a simple agreement of a horizontal type, but a conforming of all wills to that of the Lord in a mutuality of commitment which results in oneness of heart and life, in a psychic unity. Community is not formed simply by a self-propelled will: "Now I shall love my neighbor." It is rather: "I love my neighbor because I am utterly committed to God who first loved us all." In such a conception of society, the chief of the sins, the unforgivable sin, is idolatry. That is not simply because the First Commandment as law has been broken. Rather, disloyalty, ingratitude, rebellion against the Lord break the covenant unity. It is the Lord's will and blessing which create and sustain the community. If he is denied, what is there left, except a chaos of broken commitment? A shattered community which in seeking to repair the damage inaugurates the worship of creature rather than Creator. Hence all sin, no matter how inward and personal, is social sin. It has social consequences because the psychic unity of souls is broken in some measure and society is dissolved. "Vanity" or "emptiness" is an interesting word in the Biblical vocabulary for sin. This is the product of a chaotic soul which "cannot work anything, but only dissolve,"[3] which cannot love and thus link itself to the community, but only make the heart hard or the neck stiff and thus disrupt community.

Since community is a product of mutuality of commitment in

[3] Johs. Pedersen, *Israel I–II* (Oxford, 1926), p. 413; see further pp. 263 ff.

the Lord, there is a point at which loving tolerance, which characterizes the inner life of the individuals, must cease. That point is where the Lord is denied. Both the Old and New Testaments are explicit on this point. Any teacher or prophet who has all the marks of the Spirit, but who entices to idolatry, to other gods, or to that not learned in Christ, is false and a betrayer. It may be that at this point our modern tolerance, which is a great good, has betrayed us. If not, then one must ask why our churches are so man-centered instead of being God-centered? Why are they held together more by exterior organization and promotional programs than by inner commitment to God? Is it accidental that some of our fanatical fringe groups, binding themselves to the Spirit, have experienced more about some phases of Christian community than have we?

3. A third characteristic of the Biblical community has already been mentioned: that is its sense of election, of being called. Somehow or other, the idea of election has been shifted from its Biblical concentration on God's call to a special vocation into the concern with heaven and hell at death. We forget that when the apostle Paul commanded us to work out our own salvation, for it is God who works in us both to will and to work for his good pleasure (Phil. 2:12–13), he is speaking about the Christian's calling or elect vocation in this world.

Let us recall for a moment the major conversions recorded in the Bible. What, for example, is the central point in the story of the great experience of Moses? Is it the burning bush? But that was simply to attract Moses' attention. Is it the words: "Put off your shoes . . ."? But surely it is rather: "Moses, come now, I send you to Pharaoh that you may bring forth my people . . . out of Egypt" (Ex. 3:10). Or what of the great experience of Isaiah? Is the important point solely the prophet's feeling of God's holiness and his own sin? Are those scholars correct who try to derive Isaiah's theology, his whole knowledge of God, from this one great experience? I say, rather, that the central and climactic verse of that sixth chapter of Isaiah is the eighth: "And I heard the voice of the Lord saying: 'Whom shall I send, and who will go for us?' Then I said: 'Here am I. Send me.' And he said: 'Go. . . .'" Similarly in the call of Jeremiah, the central words are: "I appointed you a prophet to the nations . . . to all to whom I send you you shall go" (Jer. 1:5, 7). And finally in the conversion experience of Paul on the Damascus Road the Lord's words are: "Rise and enter the city, and you will be told what you are to do." And to Ananias the Lord said: "Go, for he [Paul] is a chosen instrument of mine to carry my name before the gentiles and kings and the sons of Israel . . ." (Acts 9:6,15).

Note the frequent occurrence in these widely separated passages of the words "send," "go," "do." The experience of God conveyed no complete theology, no statement of abstract doctrines, no precious feelings that were cherished for years hence. The experience was too awful to be sentimentalized, to be made either pretty or petty. It was rather God's way of turning a man around in his tracks and confronting him with his job. "Here is the way! Walk in it!" "Here is your work. Go, do it!"

Yet the awareness of a calling, of being sent to do something, comes in and through a community of life. The knowledge of the Biblical God is not formed in us in our solitariness. It is not a private or mysterious something which one treasures within. Knowledge is not conveyed or communicated apart from a social form or structure of thought and experience. In the Bible that form is the covenant society, and the knowledge of God is communicated in and through that form.

Every religion, I believe, has such a form through which knowledge is communicated. In Hinduism, for example, I am told that the central structure is the wheel of Karma. Together with it is the law of Dharma which is the law of the society or caste in which one is placed. To keep this law is self-fulfillment, for knowledge *is* self-fulfillment, and by this knowledge one hopes to get off the wheel of Karma in a future existence. In the ancient polytheism of Mesopotamia with its focus of attention on the integration of society with nature, the universe was conceived as a cosmic state ruled by the adjustment of many divine wills to another. Man was the slave of this state, and the knowledge of the divine world was communicated to him as to a slave through a variety of rites and through the struggle for existence in nature.

In Israel, too, the universe was conceived as a cosmic state, ruled, however, by one divine will. The world is in rebellion against this great Lord who is in the midst of the struggle to make it his faithful kingdom. Meanwhile he has formed a new society in this earth as a foretaste of the goal.

In other words, God is presented to us primarily in the form of a Ruler who is doing definite things. He is a *King in warfare* to make the world his Kingdom. He is the *King as judge,* trying people and nations for their rebellion against his rule. He is the *King as Lord, Shepherd, and Father* of his new community, which he has formed and with which he struggles to the end that it become his faithful steward or agent.

The pattern of the new society also had a definite picture behind it which gave a structure of meaning to human existence. That picture was derived from the conception of covenant, a term borrowed from law. Covenant was then and still is a treaty between two legal communities sealed by an oath or vow. The particular type of covenant that originally lay behind the Biblical doctrine of society has only recently been discovered by Professor George E. Mendenhall of the University of Michigan.[4] It is to be found in the suzerainty treaties of the second

---

[4] See *The Biblical Archaeologist,* Vol. XVIII, No. 3 (Sept. 1954); and *Law and Covenant in Israel and the Ancient Near East* (Pittsburgh, 1955).

millennium B.C. This is a treaty between a great king and his vassal. A suzerain is not a king among other kings. He is king of kings and lord of lords, who grants his covenant to his vassal. In the treaty he speaks to his vassal in the first person and describes his benevolent acts. Thus the vassal is to obey him, not because he has to, but because the great king has been so good to him. And the first requirement of the vassal is to serve the great king and him alone; a vassal state then, as now, is prohibited from having foreign relations with other powers.

This type of covenant originally provided the picture, the form, or structure, through which the knowledge of God was communicated in the Bible. God was there known as the great Suzerain whose benevolent acts toward his newly created community were to lead this people to serve him through love. No other divine powers could be honored, for these would weaken the central commitment. And the service was one of freedom. The general obligations were cast in absolute form; within the framework they provided the vassal was free to order his own life. The Ten Commandments have sometimes been objected to because several are negative, "Thou shalt not." Yet, as Professor Mendenhall has pointed out, the negative is the only truly universal form of law. A prohibition forbids action in one area, while leaving all other areas free. A positive law limits all action to the one area prescribed, thus preventing freedom of decision unless the law is so general that it provides nothing more than a frame of reference. One of the great struggles in both the Old and New Testaments was against the attempt to interpret the detailed positive law of the legal community as the constitutional law of the divine Suzerain—something which happened in Judaism.

These remarks, I realize, are to some extent cryptic. Yet the main point I am here making is that the knowledge of God in the Bible was communicated through a definite social or political form with its own particular language to describe the nature of God and the meaning of our human lives. In this structure of thinking the emphasis is not on some pious, private, or esoteric experience of the Great King. One does not speak of "experiencing" a king. Instead, our focus of attention is upon a knowledge of the Lord's will, on our attachment to him for what he has done, and on our loyalty to him in all that we do. The Lord has placed a vocation before his society, and each member hears God's command addressed to him personally.

My description here has been drawn from the Old Testament, because it provides the key to the New. The essentials of this conception of the meaning of our lives under God have actually been fulfilled and realized in Christ. God has made Christ the Head, the King, of this community, and to live in it is to live "in Christ," to love him and serve him loyally.

It is only in this setting that we can understand the peculiarly Biblical conception of "knowledge" as related to God.

One sentence that occurs again and again in the Old Testament, and one that is picked up and used especially in Ezekiel, is to the effect that such-and-such happened that "ye [or they] may know that I am the Lord." Conversely, sinners and idolaters are the way they are precisely because they do not know the Lord (Ps. 14:4; 53:4; Isa. 45:20). What is involved in this frequent use of the verb "know"? To know or not to know the Lord certainly does not have in emphasis belief in a set or prescribed creed or series of propositions, important though they may be as a guide to knowledge. Rather "to know the Lord" is to acknowledge that he is the Sovereign, that he is the Ruler who claims, and has a right to claim, our obedience because of all that he is and has done. When Isaiah 11:9 says that "the earth shall be full of the knowledge of the Lord as the waters cover the sea," he is speaking of the day when God's Kingdom will have come, when his rule will be acknowledged and obeyed. When the same prophet says: "The ox knows its owner and the ass its master's crib, but Israel does not know . . ." (1:3); or when Hosea says: "There is no faithfulness nor loyalty and no knowledge of God in the land; there is swearing, lying, killing, stealing and committing adultery" (4:1–2)—they are speaking about a special kind of knowledge. It is not simply a set of facts, truths, good ideas, or private experiences. It is rather a revealed knowledge of God's Lordship which has established a personal relationship to him, and which requires obedience. Hence those who know God will create and sustain community; those who do not know him will destroy community.

If I may paraphrase Rudolph Bultmann,[5] the conception of knowledge is conditioned by the importance and the claim of the Known. Reality is not conceived as eternal being or the timeless forms and form-giving principles which always are and ever will be. Reality is what happens in time. And this is not a series of processes related simply by cause and effect. What happens in time are the acts of God or of man under God and in response to Him. God is not thought of as a being who always is and whose existence is to be argued about one way or another; he is known as the Will who has a determined aim, who judges, is gracious, who requires. Knowledge, then, is not of God's eternal being but of his claim upon us. It is thus the reverent and obeyed acknowledgment of God's power, of his grace and requirement. So knowledge is not a private, inner possession of the knower. Man has knowledge only when he obeys, only when he acts in obedience. The theoretical life of the philosopher or theologian and the mystical experiences of those seeking religious experience are far removed from this conception. Knowledge involves the movement of the will, so that not to know is not an error to be corrected by more good ideas; it is a guilt, a rebellion.

[5] *Theologisches Wörterbuch zum Neuen Testament,* I, pp. 697–98.

The knowledge of God in the prophets is thus closely akin to the fear of God (cf. Isa. 11:2): reverent acknowledgment of God's power, of his claim, which leads one to practice brotherly love, justice, and righteousness.

V

One way of conceiving the Biblical doctrine of individual and community is to understand the nature of historical purpose as a series of interlaced or intersecting arches. The purpose of God overarches all of time. God's purpose in history is being accomplished by means of his election of a people. The time of this people is that needed to fulfill its election; the people's purpose is a portion of divine purpose; its arch is within and organically related to that of God. At the same time the community election overarches the time allotted to each individual of the community. Individuals likewise have their election, but it is within the temporal arch given the community. The time, the purpose, the task (i.e., the arch) of each person thus forms a part of the community purpose which overarches all components within it. At the same time, however, the individual arches are unique, separate, and structurally important, not only because they are vital components of the larger community arch, but because by a mystery of the divine Architect they too are tied into, organically related, to the larger span of God.

Of course, the value of any figure is limited, but this one may suggest the complexity of the Biblical organism, wherein community election is primary and a portion of divine purpose, and where within the community election each individual finds his role. Yet the individual election is likewise divinely given and divinely related; it indicates man's social nature and community calling, but it also signalizes his individual responsibility before

God. The people of God and the man of God thus find their status under God in an organism of considerable complexity.

In our time, considering the lostness of individual man, his lack of meaning in daily work, the separation of piety and the daily task, I can think of no more relevant proclamation than this concerning the Christian community and its work. The real issue, for example, is not how we can get the layman to work hard for the program of the Church, because the real program of the Church should be precisely how to help the layman be a Christian in his daily work, how to discover vocation and calling in the daily task.

Now, then, does this Biblical conception of man in society answer the question with which we began? The problems involved in the situation in Africa are too complex to make a simple answer possible. Furthermore, the Biblical conception of man in society is not to be applied to the modern problem as a poultice might be applied to a boil, with the assumption that a solution can automatically be secured from the application. Nevertheless, it must be said that the Biblical conception is certainly relevant to the situation in Africa and would do much to alleviate the severity of the problem. Its central concern is with community, and to enter this new community means a radical break with the past and with the older society. The tribe would indeed be broken. But there is something to take its place, a new community in which each person finds his calling under God, a new ethic of obedience, a new conception of the holy, a light instead of darkness.

The worship of the Lord who is not a creature, a worship centered, not in private or individualistic piety, but in historical memory and interpretation of an activity which has saved and created community, the psychic unity of life which is God's blessing upon that community committed to him, and the vocation given the new society in which each committed person

55

finds the meaning of his own life and daily work—these are the chief elements in the Biblical conception of man and society. And as one who is already committed, I myself would say that I cannot see how true society can be achieved on any other basis. Here is a neglected, yet central, part of Biblical theology which is a challenge to us in the Church. Here is what the real business of the Church is, its commission, vocation, and proclamation in the world. Biblical theology stands or falls by this doctrine of society, and for my part the theology which is not centered in it is evading the Bible and its crucial challenge to us in this day of social disruption.

4

GOD AMIDST HIS PEOPLE:
THE STORY OF THE TEMPLE

On the façade of a Greek Orthodox Church in Baltimore four Greek words are deeply engraved:

οἶκος Θεοῦ, πύλη οὐρανοῦ (*oikos theou, pule ouranou:* "house of God, gate of heaven").

The source is the Septuagint translation of Genesis 28:17, Jacob's dream at Bethel, when the Patriarch awoke and exclaimed: "How awesome is this place! This is none other than the house of God, and this is the gate of heaven."

What do these words mean to a worshiper in Baltimore today? Surely, not very much more than that "this is a house dedicated to God, and to the mysteries of his worship. Here is the gate, the open door, to the heavenly spheres, away from the turmoil of the world in which we live." That, however, is a very extended

59

eisegesis, almost, shall we say, a demythologized version of the passage. The words themselves point back beyond their present context to a deeper, hidden meaning, one which might possess a fascinating story if we were able seriously to penetrate it.

In the Genesis account of Jacob's dream, the narrator makes it quite evident that we are not to regard it simply as an inner spiritual struggle of a soul for faith. It was not written to be spiritualized, as we would like to interpret it in the modern Church. The significance of the story is rather seen in a much more external and objective light. It is conceived as an actual event in which God reveals himself to the third generation of the Fathers of Israel, as the Patriarch leaves his home. At that moment God repeats to him the promises made to Abraham. Here was the occasion when Jacob, the father of Israel, accepted the promise of the Lord and entered into a close relationship with him by responding with vows of his own. A stone was erected, according to ancient custom, to stand as a memorial of the theophany and its concrete results in establishing the relationship. Jacob's own feelings of awe are expressed in language which was calculated to impress on the reader the fact that from this time forth that spot was a special, a sacred place, sacred to the memory of the covenant made to the Father of twelve tribes of Israel. Indeed, the narrative reached its present form at a time between the late tenth and eighth centuries, when Bethel was the main holy shrine, the sanctuary sponsored by the royal court, in the (northern) Israelite kingdom. This story was a treasured memory in that kingdom because it related the event which made Bethel a special holy place, to be remembered above all others for its own sacred history, older than Sinai, older and surely more legitimate, it could be argued, than Jerusalem. Hence the memory of Jacob's dream is related in such a way as to make clear that this began Bethel's history as a holy site with a special sanctuary of its own. The words, "this is none other than the house of God; this is the gate of heaven," are thus words of the sanctuary's institution; they refer to the ancient temple, for it is from the language of ancient temple worship that the words are derived.

But what did they mean? In what sense was a small temple or shrine at Bethel "the house of God, the gate of heaven"? To reply to such a difficult question requires that we pause to examine something of the theology of the ancient pagan temple, the temple among the polytheists of the day. Israel's Jerusalem temple and the temple at Bethel were conscious adaptations of a pagan institution. This included the direct borrowing of theological symbolism in both cases. There is a great wealth of evidence in this regard for the Solomonic temple, and the Bethel temple's golden bull, so excoriated by Amos and Hosea as rank polytheism, was originally a well-known Canaanite podium for a god's statue, symbolizing, evidently, strength and active power.

I

From Egyptian and Mesopotamian archaeology we are now informed that the ancient polytheist took the phrase, "house of God" in a far more original and literal sense than it can possibly have been understood on the façade of the Baltimore church. The ancient Near Eastern world had no special term such as "temple" for the sacred edifice. It was simply a *"house"* of such and such a deity, or a *"holy place"* (*miqdash*), or a *"palace"* (Heb. *hekal* from Sumerian *e-gal*, "great house"). That is, the deity was thought to "live" or "dwell" in a house or palace in a way directly suggested by the dwelling of a king or noble. The ancient temple was a kind of manor house in which a great lord or lady resided and where he or she was served by his or her retinue of servants.

In early Mesopotamia a god could be conceived as owning a whole district. In the Babylonian creation story man was created as the slave of the gods, a menial who was to do the work of the world which the gods did not wish to do. (We may digress a moment to recall what Israel did with the same theme. In Genesis 1–3 and in Psalm 8, it could be inferred, man was also created as a slave of God. But the emphasis is not on man's slavery but on his kingship. Because of the acknowledged goodness of God, the world is God's creation and it is great and wondrous. And, of all God's creatures, it is man who is accorded a status just below that of the angels, with power and freedom to rule.)

The Babylonian creation myth appears to reflect the economy of the early Sumerian state in which the temple could be all-powerful and in possession of much of the land. In such a situation most of the people who worked the god's lands were indeed serfs, slaves of the estate. It may be recalled that writing appears first in Mesopotamia at the end of the fourth millennium B.C. But it was not invented as a boon to cultural expression, but solely to facilitate the handling of the temple's complex business.

In keeping with the idea that human beings were menial servants, each temple office in Mesopotamia was conceived to be under the supervisory control of a divine official: whether the doorkeeper, chief butler, armorer (or weapon-keeper), counselor who presents prayers and petitions from the city, footman, who brings messages, chamberlain, chariot-keeper and donkey-keeper, goatherd, musician, overseer of lands and canals, inspector of fisheries, forester, or policeman—all were actually gods with human officials (slaves) under them.

Thus in Mesopotamia there was no sharp separation between the earthly and heavenly. There was *one world*, not two, in which the gods were active. The great deities owned great estates, and lived on them in palaces (temples) with a family, wife, children, and servants. The ordinary worshiper approached the temple as a serf would approach the palace of his lord. He wanted a favor; he brought a gift; he sought an answer in an omen or dream. Thus, he got his orders, or at least an answer. The temple complex had at its center a room where the god sat enthroned, where he received visitors, issued orders, listened to petitions, settled disputes, and at mealtimes presided over the family banquet. Other rooms and buildings were erected around the central structure as they were needed and in accordance with the wealth of the establishment. As a centralized state came into being, the Babylonian temple plan was changed to emphasize the royal features: a great throne in a splendid audience hall, framed by a series of ornate doorways to give the impression of depth, awe, and majesty. In Assyria, on the other hand, the old house form was continued and simply elaborated. In Egypt, where a chief effort was expended to show that nothing ever really changed, the old, primitive cella, or sacred hut, was always kept; it was simply hidden deeper and ever deeper in the maze of courts and colonnades, so that the more advanced and complex the society, the more the chief gods, like the incarnate god who was the king (Pharaoh), were removed, hidden away, inaccessible to the ordinary worshiper.

The literalized understanding of the "house of God" meant a fairly literal anthropomorphism was not only believed by the unsophisticated, but encouraged and nourished by the whole temple institution. The god was thought to have the same needs as man: thus his physical needs of food, drink, clothing, and housing were carefully looked after. In other words, "sacrifices and offerings" represented the exploitation of natural resources by the landed aristocracy (the gods and their human representatives) for their own needs. Hence the sacrifices, even in the Old Testament, were always exquisitely prepared as food.

In the Canaanite religious texts found at Ras Shamra in Syria there is one poetic line which, in describing a heavenly banquet, explicitly says: "The gods eat the offerings; the deities drink the offerings." The menu served daily in four meals at a great temple establishment at Erech (Uruk) in Babylonia has been preserved.[1] The day began with the "Great Morning Repast," when eighteen libation jars, containing several kinds of beer, wine, and milk were served, along with eighteen sheep, one especially fine milk-fed sheep as a delicacy, one large beef, bread, dates, raisins, etc. The second breakfast, or "Small Morning Repast," was approximately the same, though with fewer sheep and the addition of various kinds of domestic fowl, birds, and eggs. The "Great Evening Repast" and the "Small Evening Repast" contained the same staples in somewhat varied amounts. One must infer that these gods at Erech, and their huge retinue of servants, had huge appetites! Like all aristocrats they were expensive and an undoubted drain on the economy.

As far as I know, the ancient polytheistic world never really spiritualized this physical view of a deity's needs, before the Greco-Roman intellectuals began to allegorize the old mythology. Yet Israel, dependent as she was, and deeply so, upon that world, and possessing her own anthropomorphism, found it necessary to set limits on that anthropomorphism. Two things in passing may be mentioned:

1. No sexuality was deemed appropriate to apply to God; he had no wife or family.

2. The idea of the Deity possessing physical needs was repulsive and could not be tolerated. Note, for example, Psalm 50:12 ff.:

[1] Thureau-Dangin, *Rituels Accadiens,* pp. 74 ff.

64

God Amidst His People

If I were hungry, I would not tell you;
for the world and all that is in it is mine.
Do I eat the flesh of bulls,
or drink the blood of goats . . . ?

The amusing story known as "Bel and the Dragon" among the
Old Testament Apocrypha is something only a Jew or a Christian
would have concocted. You will recall that it relates how Daniel
proves to the pagan king that the offerings given to the gods in
a temple were not eaten by the gods at all, but by the priests
and their families, who slipped in for a feast during the night.
Or recall Acts 17:24 f.: "The God who made the world and everything in it, . . . does not live in shrines made by man, nor is he
served by human hands, as though he needed anything, since he
himself gives to all, life and breath and everything."

But, we ask with our logical minds, how on earth could a god
dwell in a house? The original, basic feature of a great polytheistic deity was his personification of a principal or major element
in nature: sky, storm, sun, moon, Venus, earth, water, fertility,
death, etc. How could an all-pervasive or cosmic deity be
localized in a temporal, earthly building, and particularized in
a statue (the idol)? This is difficult for us to understand. The
nearest I have come to an explanation is something like this:

Basic to temple worship in polytheism was the principle that
"like" is in some measure the same as *"what"* it is like. The dream
and reality cannot be distinguished. Or act out the part of a god
in a drama, and one becomes that god in effect while he is doing
so. The likeness shares in the reality and cannot be distinguished
from it. As for the temple, it was filled with cosmic symbolism
so that it became a microcosm of the macrocosm. It reflected the
universe in which the Deity lived. One scholar has written: "Its
ceiling [of the Egyptian temple] is painted blue for the sky and
is studded with a multitude of golden stars . . . The floor . . . is

similarly conceived as the earth out of which the plants grow."[2] The same was true in Babylonia as regards symbolism. For example, most characteristic of that country was the temple tower or *ziggurat*. Originally an artificial platform erected to raise a temple above flood-water level, in the course of time the original purpose was forgotten. The tower was made higher and higher in order to lift the temple on top of it toward the sky (cf. Gen. 11:4). The main temple was now built at the base of the tower, while the building at the top "was destined to receive the deity alighting there in its descent from heaven."[3] Hence the building, which was *like* or which *symbolized* the universe, *was* in some measure the universe. Thus a cosmic deity could "dwell" in the structure without being confined to or by it. Similarly, the idol was *like* the god; therefore, on the principle of "like is like," the god and the idol are identical; one can meet the god "face to face" as he appears before the idol. Yet that can be said without the idol in any way so particularizing the Deity that he was confined to the spot where the idol was placed.

II

Turning now to the phrase "gate of heaven," one can observe immediately that the point of meeting between the divine and human worlds was not primarily in a covenant conception, as in the Bible, but in the institutions of state (kingship) and temple.

For example, the pivotal position of the temple may be indicated by the following names given to Mesopotamian temples:

[2] H. H. Nelson, *The Biblical Archaeologist*, Vol. VII, No. 3 (1944), pp. 47 f.

[3] L. Oppenheim, *ibid.*, p. 54.

"The house [which is] the link of heaven and earth"

"The house [which is] the mooring post of heaven and earth"

"The house [which is] the foundation platform of heaven and earth"

"The house [which is] the destiny [divine prefiguration] of heaven and earth."

There in the temple was the place where ultimate power was available to alleviate human need. The whole stability of the social order was dependent on the temple. For example, among the services or sacraments conducted in the temples of the Fertile Crescent three were of central importance:

1. *The New Year's Festival,* which celebrated the primordial victory of the king of the gods over the chaos dragon.
2. *The marriage* of the storm or rain god each spring to the goddess of fertility.
3. *The resurrection* of the rain and vegetation god from the death of the summer's drought each fall.

These were the great polytheistic sacraments. The creation battle had been fought and won in primordial times. Yet the chaos remains as the greatest danger to life on earth. Consequently, it must be refought and rewon. This the human king did ritually by becoming the god in a drama, and by the dramatic act making the earth safe and secure again for the coming year. King and priestess, likewise celebrating the divine marriage each spring, effected the release of the life-giving power of reproduction which nature's spring has always symbolized. But the summer's drought of the Near East was a dread time, and only the rite which brought the rain god back to life in the fall so that the rains began again —only a rite which effected a god's resurrection—brought renewal so that life could go on.

What, then, was a polytheist's sacrament? It was a dramatic action which brought about community renewal. As one scholar has put it: "By a willed act of man, was achieved divine union and in it all-pervading, life-giving, recreative potency upon which depended not only 'the life of all lands,' but even the steady flow of days and the renewal of the moon each month through the coming year."[4] By a dramatic ritual man himself, taking the part of a god, believed it possible to bring about the needed renewal of nature on which life was dependent. It was a rite to effect a result.

The very center of ancient religious life thus lay in the temple, and by means of its all-important rites man attempted to insure a gentle and steady rhythm of life and his own integration within it. Religious exaltation and excitement occurred within the rites and the exercises wherein this integration of society with nature, and the renewal of nature, was established. Heights of religious joy were not reached in non-cultic or in non-ritualized activity—such as in the Biblical "doing the will of God" or in "following the Way."

III

Turning now to Israel, we perhaps may note, in the first place, that though the sacrifices and offerings, oblations and incense, were taken over directly from the Canaanite environment for the worship of God, it would appear that the God of Israel would permit no element of sympathetic magic to be central in his worship. No cultic drama based upon the principle of "like is like" had any influence upon him. Instead the sacramen-

---

[4] Thorkild Jacobsen in V. Ferm, ed., *Dictionary of Religion* (New York, 1945), p. 485.

tal festivals were gradually reinterpreted, so that they were elevated above the processes of nature in which they had their original setting, and more and more became celebration of what God had done in choosing the Fathers, saving and forming a nation, a "people of God," at the Exodus and at Mount Sinai, and in providing them a land in which to dwell.

The historical memory involved in the festivals, and the covenantal setting in which the worship was placed provided the soil for the prophetic battle against the continued pressure to turn the worship into a rich sacramentalism and leave it at that. The central sacraments of Israel had originally been nature festivals, but they were transformed into celebrations of the mighty deeds of God. The action of the ritual was centrally to recall what God had done, and in so doing to renew community. The renewal of life lay, not in nature, but in the gracious will of God, and in man's adjustment of his will to God's will. The sacrificial cultus in its deepest meaning was not a provision for divine needs or wants to the end that a favor be wrested from a God whose attention the gift had secured. It was instead a revelation, a gift of God himself, a means which he provided whereby he might be worshiped. But let the cultus be turned into a pagan rite, conceived as efficacious in providing security—at that moment the prophet exclaimed that God hated, he despised the festivals and would have nothing to do with them. Yea, he who gave the temple would destroy it!

As for the Israelite sanctuary itself, both the nomadic tent shrine (the tabernacle) and the Solomonic temple were interpreted originally very much as pagan shrines were interpreted. They were *hab-bayt* or *beth-Yahweh*, "the house," or "the House of the Lord." They thus localized the Lord of the whole earth in the midst of his people. The Solomonic temple was filled with the same rich cosmic symbolism as were the pagan temples. The great bronze laver in the courtyard was named the "Sea," symbolizing the primeval deep, perhaps as the source of life. The great altar of burnt offering was built like a Babylonian ziggurat. Its base was named the "bosom of the earth" (Ezek. 43:14). Its top stage had four horns and was named "har' el" (Ezek. 43: 15), meaning "mountain of God." The Babylonian word *ziqquratu* (ziggurat) meant "mountain peak," referring to the cosmic mountains which supported the universe.

Thus the problem of the distance and transcendence of God, and the knowledge of and desire for his nearness, was "solved" as among pagan peoples by a rich, sacramental symbolism.

But we have sufficient evidence to indicate that Israelite theology was of such a nature as to cause a conflict over these pagan temple conceptions. In what sense can the temple be conceived as a *"House of God"*? The Deuteronomic school of covenant theology, in north Israel originally, rejected the whole notion almost outright in a bold and sweeping restatement of temple theology. This is clearly seen, for example, in Solomon's prayer of dedication of the temple, a prayer which the Deuteronomic historian has expanded so that it conveys the thought of his tradition (I Kings 8:27–30): "But will God really dwell upon the earth? Behold, neither the heavens nor the heaven of heavens can contain thee; how much less this house that I have built! Yet do thou turn unto the prayer of thy servant and to his supplication, O Lord my God . . . that thine eyes may be open toward this house night and day, even toward the place whereof thou hast said, 'My name shall be there . . .' And do thou hearken unto the supplication of thy servant and of thy people Israel, when they shall pray toward this place. Yea, hear thou in heaven thy dwelling place; and when thou hearest, forgive."

This is a clear rejection of the whole attempt to localize God or to consider his temple as a dwelling. The temple instead is simply a place where God's *name* abides. Of course, the conception of "the Name" has a long history in the ancient world. Name and essence were so intermingled that in pagan settings the two could be completely identified or the name in its own right could be separated and given mythological significance and reverenced. Yet in the setting of Deuteronomic theology there can be no doubt that the idea of the name in connection with the temple was used to separate the building's significance entirely from the priestly attempt to explain God's presence in terms of "dwelling." The temple is important, not because it is God's house in any literalized sense, but because it is God's gracious condescension to human need. It symbolizes his nearness, and provides the assurance that prayers directed toward it will be heard and answered. The temple was a house of prayer in this theology; we are thus provided a bridge to the synagogue worship of the later day (cf. also Isa. 56:7).

The Jerusalem priesthood countered this theology with their own refinement of the old dwelling idea. As Frank M. Cross, Jr., was the first to point out,[5] they chose an old, archaic word for "tent" that was no longer in common use (*shakan*) for all references to God's "dwelling" on earth. A man may *dwell* (*yashab*) in a house, but God never "dwells" as man does. He dwells (*yashab*) only in heaven. On earth God is said only "to tent," or "tabernacle" (*shakan*). Indeed, the whole wonder of God's dealings with Israel lies in the assertion that he has chosen "to tabernacle" in the midst of his people. Insofar, or as long as that is the case, Israel will be a people of God. When Ezekiel, the prophet from the Jerusalem priesthood, presented the Babylonian destruction of Judah, he did so by seeing it as a divine act, carried out by divine messengers, after the Glory of the Lord had left the temple. In the new day, on the other hand,

---

[5] See his remarks in *The Biblical Archaeologist*, Vol. X, No. 3 (Sept. 1947), pp. 65–68.

there will be a new people and a new temple, to which the Glory will return (Ezek. 9–11, 44:4).

Scholars have been inclined to interpret the priestly view as a crass statement of the divine immanence and particularism. Yet the vocabulary used became a technical one for describing solely the wonder and mystery of God's earthly presence amongst his people for purposes of revelation and atonement.

In neither the Deuteronomic school nor in the Jerusalem priesthood can the cosmic and omnipotent God be confined to an earthly sanctuary. Yet a means must be found to express the certainty of his presence in the covenant relationship whereby those who had been slaves became a people. The Deuteronomic school interpreted this in an almost completely non-sacramental, non-priestly manner. The Jerusalem priesthood was interested in the sacramental or cultic presence of God in the people's worship for purposes of self-revelation and forgiveness of sins.

It is of interest to note that the terminology of the priests in Jerusalem is present in the New Testament, though sometimes hidden in translation: for example:

Jn. 1:14.   *The Word became flesh and tented* [English *dwelt*] *among us.*

Heb. 8–9.   Christ as high priest has entered the true tent (which is not the earthly copy but heavenly original) and offers, not sacrifices, but himself.

Rev. 21:2–3.   *The new Jerusalem came down from heaven . . . , "and I heard a great voice from the throne saying, 'Behold the tabernacle of God is with men, and he will tabernacle with them and they shall be his people . . .'"*

It is no longer a building, but Christ himself who is our tabernacle, that is the Presence who has created us a people of God, and will sustain us in the same.

IV

A few remarks in conclusion:

In the breakup of the Israelite and Judean state with the scattering of the Jews in the world, the synagogue institution developed. Unlike the old temple the synagogue was a building into which people entered, were seated, studied the Law, sang and prayed together. As a religious institution its difference from other sacred structures was profound, because the people's theology made it so.

It was in the atmosphere of the synagogue, then, that the Church developed. Christian meetings were held first in homes, and then in separately constructed buildings, but they were congregational meetings, and the buildings where they were held reflected this viewpoint. The theology of the structure was originally drawn from the setting of the covenant theology (which centered precisely in God's creating a people or congregation).

At this point a new story should begin: "The Story of the Church," but this is a subject which is not within my specific competence. Perhaps, however, I may be permitted a few fairly obvious remarks:

Is it not true that the developing Catholic Church seriously attempted to draw on the priestly ideas of the Old Testament far more, of course, than was done in the New Testament itself, and in so doing to fulfill in the Church the old temple theology of the Jerusalem priesthood? Hence the Church became a temple, in a sense, holy because of the *real* presence of Christ within it. Yet there was now a non-Biblical twist, a magical element from the old "like-is-like" formula. That appeared in the transubstantiation of the elements by a rite of man, and the effecting of atonement by a little drama, in which the events of the New Testament are re-enacted. Hence a priest offers upon an altar the sacrifice of Christ to God for us, and each time wins for us anew the blessings of atonement. Am I right in thinking that the basis of this resembles much more the pagan sacrament than it does the Biblical sacrament? The mass is not a covenant ceremony in which historical memory and new commitment play the dominant part, but in common practice it seems rather to be a drama conducted to *effect a result.*

Protestantism rejected the mass, and with it the whole temple theology as thus carried over into the Church. This meant a reinterpretation of the meaning of the edifice of worship, such as happened in the Deuteronomic theology. A new design for the building was needed, except in the Anglican compromise. Yet today there is considerable confusion on this issue among Protestants, certainly little clarity, and careful and continued discussion of the problem would appear by no means unprofitable. What is the meaning of a church edifice? In what sense is it "the house of God, the gate of heaven"? The solution is certainly not to be found by turning one's back on the whole history of the subject. For the Protestant Christian, it would appear to this speaker at least, the solution must lie in the New Testament's reinterpretation of the Deuteronomic "house of prayer" and the priestly "tabernacle." The church is both the house of prayer and the place where we celebrate the Presence of the living Christ in our midst, the Presence which has made us a people.

Yet how is that Presence effectively real in our midst? Catholic theology has celebrated the Real Presence by the rite of the mass in which transubstantiation is effected. The end result of the rite is community renewal by means of the miraculous Presence of him who gave himself for us. Yet what has happened to the Biblical sense of the covenant community?

The Lord's Supper was a covenant meal, the anticipatory

74

celebration of the New Covenant, the new people created by God's act in Christ. The Passover meal was transformed, as it had been among the Essenes of the Dead Sea Scrolls, into a banquet which anticipated the eschatological meal with the Messiah, who would return amongst his people in the New Creation. But with what aim and with what result do we in the Church continue to celebrate the Holy Supper?

One theological line derived from the Bible would emphasize the following:

1. The celebration of God's act in Christ in delivering us from slavery to the powers of darkness.
2. The celebration of the New Covenant which in Christ has created the Church, the people of God.
3. The renewal of our commitment to God in Christ and of our vows to live in love and in brotherhood in the New Covenant.
4. The anticipation of that day toward which the Lord of history is moving, when we shall all join in the "covenant of peace," in the "banquet with the Messiah," in the hope which lies in God and not in ourselves.

When the original covenant setting is preserved and emphasized in the Biblical sense, it is not necessary to dwell on the "Real Presence" within the Church. To do so is to miss the point. Covenant means "God with us." But it also means that *we* have vowed to be his people, to serve him in this world without fear. God's act is celebrated, but it is a definite act in time, which gives meaning to history and to my vocation within history.

If, however, the sacrament is celebrated as a necessary rite, repeated to effect our salvation, or rather to *make effective* now, for us, the salvation wrought by God in the primordial event, the Biblical center of the theology is missed. It is no longer primarily a covenant celebration. It becomes an almost timeless, universalized transaction, wherein our salvation is secured and insured, as it is daily or periodically repeated. And the central emphasis is not on a salvation within history, in the new community formed in Christ, but a salvation beyond history. The rite becomes a "medicine for immortality." Even in the Anglican-Episcopal service of communion, at the climax when from the Bible one would expect the words of the covenant, we instead hear these words: "The Body of our Lord Jesus Christ, which was given for thee, preserve thy body and soul unto everlasting life." The source of this theology can ultimately be traced back to the Gospel of John, though only after much reinterpretation (cf. especially John 6:52–59). The main stream of Protestant thought and practice, on the other hand, has found itself more oriented in the central stream of Biblical theology, as it is found in the Marcan and Pauline accounts of the Supper: "This cup is the New Covenant in my blood" (I Cor. 11:25; Mark 14:24).

5

SECURITY AND FAITH:
AN EXPOSITION OF JEREMIAH 7:1-15

The Hebrew of Jeremiah 7:1–15 may be translated somewhat as follows:

The word which came to Jeremiah from the Lord, saying:
Stand in the gate of the Lord's house and proclaim there this
word: And you shall say: Listen to the word of the Lord all
Judaeans who enter these gates to worship the Lord. Thus
saith the Lord of Hosts, God of Israel: Reform your ways
and your doings and I shall abide with you in this place. Do
not rely on the lying words, The Temple of the Lord, The
Temple of the Lord, The Temple of the Lord [Heb. "Temple of Yahweh—these!"].

Now if you *really* reform your ways and your doings, if
you *really* do justice between man and man, [if] the so-

79

journer, the orphan, and the widow are *not* oppressed, [if] innocent blood you do not shed in this place, and after other gods you do not walk to your hurt, then I will abide with you in this place, in the land which I gave your fathers from of old and unto eternity.

But behold, you are relying on lying words without success. Will you steal, murder, commit adultery, swear falsely, burn incense to Baal, and go after other gods whom you've not known, then come and stand before me in this house, which is called by my name, and say: *We are saved,* simply to continue doing all these abominations? Has this house which is called *by my name* become a hide-out for oppressors in your eyes? Yea, I myself have seen it, saith the Lord!

But, I pray you, go to my sanctuary which was in Shiloh, where I caused my name to abide in the early days. See what I did to it because of the evil of my people Israel. *And* NOW—because you do all these deeds, saith the Lord—even though I have continuously and persistently spoken to you, and you would not listen, though I called you and you would not answer—I shall do to the house which is called by my name and in which you rely, yea to the place which I gave to you, and to your fathers, just what I did to Shiloh. And I shall throw you out from me, just as I threw out all your brethren, even the whole progeny of Ephraim.

I

HISTORICAL SETTING

A. This is a prose summary preserved by the disciples of Jeremiah of a sermon delivered at one of the great temple festivals, probably either Passover or Tabernacles, in the year

608 B.C. In chapter 26 Jeremiah's biographer gives the story of what happened as a result:

The religious leaders in the temple were so angered by what Jeremiah had said that they stirred up a mob scene, accused Jeremiah of blasphemy, and cried out for his death.

So violent were the emotions and accusations that a royal commission of judges, composed evidently of government officials, rushed from the palace, and sat in judicial assembly to try the case. There the accusation was made, Jeremiah gave his defense, and the court said in its verdict that Jeremiah was not worthy of the death penalty. The precedent cited was the case of Micah, who a hundred years before had prophesied something similar. Yet King Hezekiah had not put him to death, but instead had hearkened, prayed, and received God's forgiveness.

A final paragraph, however, tells of another prophet, Uriah, who had said the same things, had fled to Egypt for safety, but was extradited by King Jehoiakim and slain. Jeremiah was saved because of one high official, a man named Ahikam (26:24), from one of Jerusalem's most prominent families.

Our question, then, is this: What was it about Jeremiah's address that made the religious leaders so terribly angry?

At this point we must pause for historical background to find the setting for the sermon. The greatest event in the years preceding the address had been the fall of Nineveh, and before that the gradual decline of the Assyrian Empire. In the 620's a great Judean king by the name of Josiah, a second David, had gradually, step by step, freed his country from the Assyrian yoke as the empire weakened, and then in 622 B.C., on the basis of an old lawbook found in the temple (as we all know, Deuteronomy or some portion thereof), had carried out a great reform. This reform was conducted not only in Judah but also in Israel. A united state of Palestine had come into being for the first time since the days of Solomon. The whole country was reformed on the basis of that understanding of the old Mosaic covenant—apparently long since forgotten among most Judeans—as is provided in the core of the Book of Deuteronomy.

Then with the fall of Nineveh in 612, the Pharaoh of Egypt decided that it was time to intervene in the affairs of Asia. If he could come to the support of that remnant of the Assyrian army which had taken refuge in the north Mesopotamian provinces, he might create a buffer between himself and the rising power of Babylon, and thus with little trouble take over the old Egyptian Syro-Palestinian empire.

What was Josiah to do? This was a terrible dilemma. Certainly freedom for Judah and his own aspirations for a new kingdom of David were threatened. He decided to "bet," as it were, on the more distant power of Babylon, and if, when the Egyptian army was on its way to northern Syria, he could keep that army from getting there in time, he might well win in the end. Hence in the spring of 609 B.C. he put his little army across the pass of Megiddo, forced the Egyptians to deploy and carry on a costly siege of the city of Megiddo. Thus he accomplished his purpose. The Egyptian army did not reach northern Syria in time to prevent the Assyrian collapse to the Babylonians. But in that battle Josiah was slain.

Here, then, was the end of the era, the downfall of all new hopes and dreams. Pharaoh Necho took over the kingdom of Judah. He deposed that son of Josiah whom the people wanted. He put on the throne a young scoundrel, another son, whose throne name was Jehoiakim. Had all God's promises in the great reform of Josiah been in vain? Is this the answer of God to reform and obedience?

At that critical juncture in the affairs of the nation it appears that the priests and the popular cult prophets of the Jerusalem temple laid plans for a great religious revival. They coined a new slogan: "Here is the Temple of the Lord." And they had excellent precedent. A hundred years before, the prophet Isaiah had said that Zion would not be destroyed by the Assyrian army. It had not been destroyed; it was saved.

II
JEREMIAH'S MESSAGE

A. There is a deceptive sincerity about the priests' call for a religious rally. Is not the Lord's house the nation's one bulwark? Did not Isaiah say that one cannot depend upon horses and chariots, upon armaments and treaties for security? Is there not demanded of us a bold faith which against all appearances to the contrary affirms the invisible realities symbolized in the House of the Lord? What has stood firm, century by century, weathering all storms and calamities? It is the House of God. Let us rally around it, take our religious duties more seriously, attend the services regularly, cultivate faith with sacrifice, prayer, and generous gifts. Here is your stronghold when the foundations are shaking.

Now what is the difficulty with this call? In what way does it differ from what we might say?

Yet Jeremiah dared pick a day when a vast throng was present at divine service—not a private audience of a few friends with words spoken gently, but a great public assembly with words spoken harshly. In a voice that could probably be heard throughout the whole throng, he called the priestly program a lie and a delusion:

"Do not put any confidence in the priest's babblings about the Temple of the Lord, the Temple of the Lord, the Temple of the Lord. They are lying words."

Instead of the priestly slogan Jeremiah coined a new one: "Amend your ways, reform your doings, and God will abide with you here." But put no trust in these pious lies you are hearing.

Recall Job's challenge to his friends: "Will you speak a falsehood for God? For him will you mouth deceit?" (Job 13:7).

This is a surprising and shocking, almost impious, thrust. How dare that gloomy misfit of a prophet, so full of personality maladjustments that even the best psychiatrist would have been overwhelmed—how dare such a one call us liars in the most intimate and sincere aspirations of our piety? If God's house is not a people's bulwark, what is?

But the prophet replies: You lie for God! Do you think the end justifies any means, even pious falsehoods? To protect yourselves and your jobs and your institutions, will you lie to the people and tell them that God's new life movement is "church" attendance and expansion? Will your evangelism save our country? Do you not know what Isaiah really said: that God hates all your religiosity, your pious, religious exercises, your ecclesiastical folde-rol, when you have no equal concern for common justice and morality in our society? What good is prayer, and temple, and sacraments when your common life is what it is! You lie, and you have made this people to believe a lie!

B. The priests are promising the people of God security, based upon the presence of God in their midst, a presence whose sign is the temple. Jeremiah's reply is cast somewhat in the form of a legal brief, such as one would use in a court of law.

1. First the statement of the case (vv. 3–4): Reform your ways and God will abide with you, but do not trust the falsehoods of the priests.

2. Then follows the review of what God actually did promise, as it should properly be understood. *If* you reform your ways and actually do justice between man and man and do not serve other masters, then God will indeed abide with you. That is his promise, but those are his conditions.

84

3. Next (vv. 8–11) we have the indictment, a direct accusation of gross social and corporate sin. The Ten Commandments seem to lie back of this indictment: taking the Lord's name in vain (swearing falsely), theft, murder, adultery, and idolatry.

Does a people dare violate openly and flagrantly the basic commandments of God, and then piously stand before God in his house and say: "We are saved! Here we are safe!"?

4. So obvious is the answer to this question that the trial proceedings are not mentioned further, but in verses 12–15 the judicial sentence is passed, introduced by the example of Shiloh, where an earlier sanctuary had been destroyed by the Philistines in the time of Samuel. Because the people have not hearkened, the sentence read: (a) the Temple, the seal of security, will be destroyed, and (b), furthermore, the people will be dispersed and scattered.

Here, then, is a terribly serious and solemn indictment that strikes directly at the root of some of our most cherished illusions.

We note two things in particular: (a) The perennial attempt of the religious man to separate piety from the common life. (b) The reliance on God's house as a place to run for safety, a kind of foxhole to which one can retreat, when evil pursues him and the foundations of security are shattered.

III

First, then, the conditional element in the promise of God's abiding presence.

The abiding presence of God in our midst, that said the priests is what makes us a people. Without that gracious presence, we are nothing, lost.

We recall here the Gospel of John with its comparable perspective: Christ "tenting" in our midst, as the Word become flesh, full of grace and truth (i.e., the Hebrew steadfast love and gracious fidelity). But does that abiding presence *promise security*, apart from the righteousness of God against all unrighteousness seen in the cross?

In the Old Testament God set conditions to his promises of rest and abiding presence. These were obedience to the purposes for which the people were placed in the Promised Land. Loving God and loving the neighbor were the sum of those conditions, but both meant more than personal decency, good will, and a desire to be nice. They meant the creation of a society in which redemptive love was the basis of economic and political life; that is, where justice to the poor and the weak prevented their exploitation, and where rectitude replaced dishonor in the various phases of the common life. So Jeremiah: What God promised was to abide with you, *if* you really do justice, *if* the weak are not oppressed, and *if* you do not give your allegiance to other gods.

A. But many of Jeremiah's hearers would have replied: We *are good* people. Sinners, yes; but no more than was Job. We *are* concerned with justice; we *do* distribute to the poor; we *do not* attend the idolatrous orgies of the paganizing high places. Why scold us like that? And Jeremiah would have replied: But you are guilty! This is your society; you cannot escape blame for it. No individual can escape involvement in the society of which he is a part. God charged us as a chosen people, and we shall bear the punishment for this iniquitous life that we as a people have developed. Look at the streets of this fair city: lying, cheating, stealing, adultery, murder upon murder! Do you think you can stand before God in this temple, and say that you are good, and therefore innocent of these crimes? We are individuals, yes—and as individuals we are to stand firm in the old ways to see the good way. But we are also a people, given a land, a good land, and with the gift goes the responsibility. Evasion of that responsibility will bring God's judgment. When there is wickedness, there is no peace; where there is gross evil, there will be blood and tears. There is no escape, unless by God's grace you emerge with your life; but expect no more.

B. Many others in the company of those who heard Jeremiah were evidently just ordinary people, who knew little about the old covenant demands of God. Like the natural man in all times and places, like so many of our Christian laymen today, they simply did not see the connection between attendance on divine worship and social justice and immorality. What is the purpose of religion, except to give comfort, a place of retreat to another world, a place of beautiful mystery, where one can turn from the crudity of the present world to a realm of beauty and forgetfulness, where ideals seem meaningful and where peaceful promises seem to be true?

Behind Jeremiah, however, is a completely different religious tradition, one in which faith and obedience are one, where life and piety are joined, where religious exaltation is not in retreat from the world into sacred courts, but in following the paths of the Lord in the world. Elijah in fear, retreating to the Lord's sacred mountain, receives no encouragement from God's challenge: "What doest thou here?" Jeremiah himself, deeply disturbed by the terrible burden placed upon him, complains of God's ways. But God's only answer is: "Jeremiah, if you have raced with men on foot, and they have wearied you, how will you compete with horses?" When Jeremiah says he will speak no more in God's name because he is met with mockery and derision on every side, then God is too strong for him, for "there is in my heart as it were a burning fire, shut up in my bones; I am weary of withholding it, I cannot!" (12:5; 20:9).

The temple is no retreat from life. Worship as a substitute for obedience is a lie.

C. Still a third group among Jeremiah's hearers were those with no inner consistency, who had followed their own desires, saw no problem in offering incense to Baal, or in any number of religious experiments, while at the same time, by fair means or foul, they were intent on accumulating all the property they could, swearing falsely, stealing, committing adultery, following other masters. And now in the new crisis of confidence, they heeded the call of the priests, adding temple attendance to their arsenal of devices for moving successfully and confidently in the world. They possessed the cards for many tricks, and if this new move provided a successful trump, fine! Added security never hurts!

To them, as to all groups, Jeremiah exclaims: How think you to come out of this iniquitous society in which you live and for which you are responsible, and stand before God in his house, and say: *We are saved*—only to go out and continue in precisely the same way as before. Has God's house become a cave, a hide-out, a place of concealment for the wicked? This is no assembly of the devout, humbly and earnestly seeking to praise the Lord, to repent, to seek forgiveness, and to leave with new resolve. You have made this temple a den of robbers, a magical fetish which you think assures you life and safety in the midst of a foul society which you have produced.

IV

The real issue in Jeremiah's sermon, then, is the question of security.

The House of God, in itself, is no guarantee of safety—this said at a time when people were anxious for security. Their religious leaders surrounded them with fatuous promises of peace,

peace—attend God's house and be saved—until Jeremiah found
this gospel his greatest enemy. "From prophet to priest," Jeremiah says, "everyone deals falsely. They have healed the wound
of my people lightly, saying peace, peace, when there is no
peace. . . . No, they were not even ashamed; they did not know
how to blush," when they said it (8:10–12).

And in the crisis which followed, the people, therefore,
"looked for peace, but no good came, for a time of healing, but
behold, terror" (8:15). And to one false prophet who said all
terror would end in two years, Jeremiah could only reply: "I will
believe it when I see it come to pass; then it will be known that
the Lord has truly sent the prophet." And the prophet was
shown to be wrong and Jeremiah right (Jer. 28).

A similar problem with regard to the temple is encountered in
the New Testament, until Stephen in his defense is led to ex-
claim: "Ye stiffnecked and uncircumcised in heart and ears, ye
do always resist the Holy Spirit" (Acts 7:51). And the new
Jerusalem of Revelation (chap. 21:22) was a city with no temple, for the presence of God and of his Christ within it were the
temple indeed.

There is a remarkable similarity between those ancient days
and ours. We, too, live at a time when the primary words are
"peace" and "security." Our people, too, are surrounded by their
prophets and priests, their cultic functionaries, who are giving
the same words of assurance in the name of the Lord as did the
religious leaders of Jeremiah's day. But in the day of terror,
where will be the peace, the comfortable adjustment to things as
they are? Is this Gospel which is called by Christ's name become
a *hiding place* for sinners? Has the Church which bears the
name of the crucified and risen Lord become a magical fetish
to which people retreat for imagined safety, while the common
life remains unchallenged, unillumined by the piercing thrust
of both Jesus and the prophets?

To quote from Professor Joseph Haroutunian:[1]

> Worship without fear or faith is the ultimate symptom of Protestant degeneracy. When men come to Church neither to confess their sins nor to hear God's Word of judgment and mercy, neither to hear God's Law nor to hear of His grace in Christ Jesus, neither to voice the cry of this body of sin and death nor to declare their hopes by faith in Him who raised Jesus from the dead, in short when they come to Church without their sin and go without forgiveness—they turn worship into vanity and religion into a spiritual farce.

> Will ye speak falsehood for God?
> For him will ye mouth deceit?

Professor Philip E. Jacob, of the University of Pennsylvania, has made a careful study of contemporary student life in the United States, under the title, *Changing Values in College* (Hazen Foundation, n.d.—1957). His summary profile of the typical American student is somewhat as follows:

A dominant characteristic of the present generation of students is that they are "gloriously contented" with regard to their day-by-day activities and future outlook, and they are "unabashedly self-centered" about it all and about the material gratifications they expect to gain in their lives in the future. They have an "easy tolerance of diversity." They are conformists themselves, and they are not going to take up a crusade for anything; for example, for non-discrimination. They will accept it if it comes as a necessary convention in a homogenized society. They respect the moral virtues that their fathers have taught them, but they do not censor, or wish to censor, those who depart from these particular canons, nor are they themselves particularly concerned with unbending consistency in this matter.

---

[1] *Wisdom and Folly in Religion* (New York, Scribner's), p. 30.

Their standards are generally low, for example, with regard to academic honesty, "systematic cheating being a common practice rather than the exception at many major institutions." The students feel a need for religion also, but it has a kind of a "ghostly quality" because it has very little to do with "the behavior of men in society, if widespread student judgment is accepted." They expect to be dutifully responsive toward government, to obey the laws, pay taxes, serve in the armed forces; but by and large they are completely irresponsible politically and often politically illiterate as well. And this disposition is reflected in strangely contradictory attitudes toward international affairs. They predict another war within a dozen years or so. Yet international problems are their least concern. Of course they set great stock by college education. Yet only a minority "seem to value their college education primarily in terms of its intellectual contribution," in its ability and power to join a person to the great stream of human culture whereby he becomes a true human being. But instead they are interested primarily in vocational preparation, and skills for that vocation which will give them the security they confidently expect to have. And our college education, says Professor Jacob, surprisingly seems to do little to change all this. Students come with these viewpoints and they leave with them.

This is the general environment out of which students come to the theological seminary to prepare for the Christian ministry. Can they or we escape from it completely? In this environment is the Church for us to be simply a place of security and safety? Will we lend our support to the current pressure to conform, to turn the Church, not into a place where sinners confess their sins, and where the redemptive love of God is heard and followed in the common life, but instead into a hiding place for sinners where they remain safe from God? In its busy and demanding activity will we find the Church enfolding us in its bosom, like an overly demanding and protective mother? Or by us will it become the vehicle for the gospel of God? Security, safety in this place, is in God alone and in our obedience to God. If we will not obey, he will destroy our temple, and ourselves with it. And if we obey, we are granted no certainties about peace, nor about the preservation of a building, nor about economic security, nor about ecclesiastical preferments. But we do become active members of God's true Church against which "the Gates of Hell" will never prevail—and for which God's holy name be praised forever and ever!

6

THE RULE OF GOD:
THE HOLY SPIRIT

Some time ago I received a letter from the editor of a medical journal in Minnesota. He said that as a layman he had been using every moment of his spare time in helping rural congregations, and that he had become very much concerned about "the Church's concern in preserving itself as an entity, regardless of its spiritual effectiveness." He continued:

> In one country church in which I worked for over two years to bring it back to enough strength to call a minister, I found the church administering to every need but the spiritual need of its members. The man who had lost a son in the war, his health through the passage of time, and wandered through his declining years without faith; the young man of great talent tied to the economic chains of family

support; the mixed marriages; the problem children; all the forms of frustration went unhelped while the Ladies Aid worked to raise money to pay for the new chairs which the Ladies Aid needed to sit on while they planned to raise money. And then a candidate for the ministry of that church asked me if I felt the church was a proper one for a liturgical revival!

The sixth Sunday after Trinity was also the third Sunday after the doctor told Mrs. Johnson her beautiful daughter was an idiot and advised an institution. The agonized searching for the power of the spirit in the name of Jesus Christ that is laying foundations for living was not in the form of a liturgy.

I have discovered in myself that when I most wish to hide from God, I can do it in the church. I can buy off the relentless demands of the Spirit by relentless efforts to promote a society.

A central question for us churchmen is this: If God through Christ is the head of the Church, just how does he rule it? None of us would care to admit that God is nothing more than a figurehead, or a mascot, which the Church carries along for sentiment only. We believe in God; we acknowledge him as our Lord; but how does he rule our Church? What role do we permit him? Is there a sense in which he is in controversy with us and our seemingly successful program? For example, when we with the highest of ideals set up a new life program, and then find it turned into a church promotion campaign because we are caught in the institutional structure, can we rest in peace and say we have obeyed our Lord's commission? When we fire the enthusiasms of young people to convert pagans to Christ, only to have them discover that their primary responsibility is to be institutional executives, have we in any sense betrayed their calling?

A few years ago there was a great investiture of cardinals in Rome which was fully reported in the American press. A writer in *Time* magazine, after giving all the details of pomp and ceremony, concluded his article with this remark: "all of which is very interesting, especially when one reads the New Testament!" To the bureaucratic promotional program of the typical major denomination today one might make the same remark. Almost instinctively the deeply converted and committed minister feels the contrast between Christ's commission and that which he is forced to spend most of his energies doing. If God actually rules and directs our great ecclesiastical bureaucracies, he is surely a greater God than most of us have ever imagined! While committed to his Gospel, we scarcely give him a chance to rule. As Karl Barth said at Amsterdam: "For just this is the final root and ground of all human disorder; the dreadful, godless, ridiculous opinion that man is the Atlas who is destined to bear the dome of heaven on his shoulders." Or as a writer in *The New Yorker* magazine wrote after the atomic bomb fell on Hiroshima: "The quest for a substitute for God ended suddenly. The substitute turned up. And who do you think it was? It was man himself, stealing God's stuff."

These rather facetious and one-sided remarks are intended solely to point up the difficulty that is felt, and always has been felt, between the Church as the new society, as the organism of God's people, and the Church as an organization in this world.

I

At the end of the last century, a German scholar, Rudolph Sohm, published a great work on Ecclesiastical Law (*Kirchenrecht*, 1892). One of his basic questions was: How did the

Catholic Church arise out of the New Testament people of God? The latter was a spiritual organism; the body of Christ was a unity, held together, united into one, by an interior spirit, the Spirit of God through Christ. Hence, the true Church was and is a spiritual unity. Catholicism, says Sohm, arose through the legalization of this unity. It is not enough to say with Harnack and others that the passage from primitive Christianity to early Catholicism took place because of the influence of Greek thought. Catholic Christianity is a legalized community with a legal constitution, and no distinction is made between the Church in a legal sense and the Church in a religious sense as the Body of Christ, between a Church completely ruled by law and one ruled charismatically, by the Spirit. Furthermore, the legal system inevitably became monarchical in form. Christ is Lord or King of the Church, and he rules through human agents, chosen and directed by his Spirit. Hence, Church officers are Christ's men, not first of all representatives of the congregation. Turn this from spiritual symbol into law, and a monarchical system results. Sohm asks: "Where is Christ, the Lord of Glory? Where the people of Christ (the *ecclesia*), in whose midst Christ is with all his spiritual gifts? Where is the visible Church? Where the true Christianity?" Everything depends upon the answer to this question. Throughout the first century, one dominant answer was maintained: "Where two or three are gathered together in my name, there am I in the midst of them." Catholicism said: "Where the bishop is (with the presbyters and deacons), there is the Catholic Church, there is the Spirit of Christ and all his benefits—*and there only*." But who is the bishop? It is he who is constituted by rite (legally); that is, elected, accepted, ordained, and inducted according to law. All other spiritual possessions of the Church were likewise legalized. "That is a valid

sacrament which is administered *rite* [according to legally ordained form] by one who is legally [by *rite*] appointed to that
ministry—all others are void of spiritual effect. Even the truth
was legalized; indeed it was primarily for the sake of an objective criterion of truth that the legal constitution was established."[1]

Sohm had a peculiar idea of law; he seemed to believe that
true religion is spiritual, and can have nothing to do with law
because law enforces, coerces, whereas the things of the spirit
cannot be coerced or confined in the frame of law. There is
much in this, but Harnack for one criticized Sohm for making
such a sharp distinction between religion and law as though
they had to do with completely separate spheres.[2] Yet Sohm was
pointing up the contrast between the charismatic organism of
the Bible and the vast legal organization which the Church
was to become, a contrast which seems to me valid and
important. "Charismatic" refers to special God-given gifts
of body and spirit which are to be used for specific tasks
in a community. These gifts are not conferred by human
acts or rites. They are either within a person or they are not;
they cannot be compelled or coerced. They are gifts of God's
grace, conferred on whom and when he sees fit. They include special powers of leadership and discernment, but they
also include the Christian virtues, faith, hope, and love. These
virtues to the Christian are unmerited gifts; they cannot
be gained by will power, by rite, or by religious education. They
are the mysterious gifts of God to those in his fellowship or

[1] Walter Lowrie, *The Church and Its Organization, An Interpretation of Rudolph Sohm's Kirchenrecht,* 1904, p. 13.

[2] Adolf Harnack, *Entstehung and Entwickelung der Kirchenverfas-
sung und des Kirchenrechts in den zwei ersten Jahrhunderten,* 1910,
pp. 155 ff.

household of faith. In other words, the Bible's view is that God rules in his community, primarily or first of all, by his charismatic gifts, given where and when he chooses. This conception dominates the Biblical portrayal of the rule of God, and to that portrayal let us now turn.

II

To understand the Bible on this point it is imperative that we begin with the Old Testament, in order to see the whole perspective. Nothing wearies me more than those attempts to teach the Bible by confining attention to the New Testament with the addition of a preliminary chapter or two on Judaism and Hellenism. The Bible is an organic whole which is the sum of neither one of its parts. In the Book of Judges we are told in the eighth chapter that, after Gideon's great victory over the raiding camel-riders, the Midianites, the men of Israel said to him: "Rule over us, you and your son and your grandson also; for you have delivered us out of the hand of Midian." Gideon said to them: "I will not rule over you, and my son will not rule over you; the Lord rules over you" (vv. 22–23).

Here was the first attempt in Israel to establish a monarchy, and it was rejected because, as Gideon said, the people already had a king who was God himself. Later on when a king was finally established, certain "reactionary" individuals did not like the idea at all. One of them in writing his version of the story preserves an old tradition that what God really said to Samuel when the people asked for a king was: "Samuel, they are not rejecting you; actually they are rejecting me from being king over them" (I Sam. 8:7).

In Israel's revealed order the affirmation that God is Lord was felt to be the most relevant political statement that one could make. While God's rule was exercised from his invisible heavenly throne, it was nonetheless effective. For one thing, he always chose human media, and made his will known to them directly or through angelic messengers. This meant that all organization and government was either of divine institution and active direction, or else useless, unprofitable, even sinful. Furthermore, any institution which once had received what appeared to be a permanent covenant and blessing could find itself in condemnation and deprived of blessing when it failed its God-given task. The conception of a direct heavenly rule meant the subjection of all human organization to it, and every promise and blessing given was contingent upon the fulfillment of election to a responsible task. Saul was chosen; then rejected. The kingdom was established; then destroyed. The cultus for worship traced its origin to the Sinai revelation; yet the divine Word by prophet and apostle proclaimed that God now despised it, had fulfilled it, and that it held no permanent status in his plans. Among the terrible words which Ezekiel heard from God were two which specially shocked him. One was the command to eat unclean food (chap. 4:13–14); the other was the divine order to "defile the house" (*i.e.*, temple; 9:7). Pious sensibilities, trained in a tradition which once had received God's sanction, meant more to man than to God. The Lord by his rule could shock and dismay; institutions and the pious feelings connected with them received no permanent "Yea" from the heavenly throne.

Israel's revealed order of society originally contemplated no kingship. God was the active King, and his rule was exercised charismatically. That is, human leaders were empowered by God's Spirit, and sent to perform specific tasks. Joshua was no son of Moses. He was a charismatic leader, as Moses himself had been. Neither the attempts of Abimelech, nor those of the sons of Eli or of Samuel, to perpetuate a political leadership in one family were successful. Gideon's affirmation to those who wished to turn his temporary, charismatic office into a monarchy preserves the ideology of the period: "I will not rule over you . . . the Lord rules over you."

David was the last of the great charismatic, political figures. Dynastic succession gave permanence and stability to the government in Jerusalem, and God's rule was now conceived to operate through a chosen king with whose dynasty he had made an everlasting covenant. The priestly office was regulated and subjected to political authority. Institutionalism replaced the freer, Spirit-led tribal association of the earlier time.

But would the sovereign God permit himself to accept a secondary position, to step into the background, while the Davidic king in possession of a permanent sanction ruled unchecked by the divine kingship? That is, would the older charismatic ideal limit the absolutism of monarchy? The crisis in government which the monarchy introduced was concerned with the rule of God. No wonder Samuel is represented as hearing God say to him: the people "have not rejected you, but they have rejected me from being king over them" (I Sam. 8:7).

Yet God continued his direct rule by charisma, by the Spirit, and the office of prophecy was the one he used. Priests and kings were ordained to office by rite, legally. But as far as we know prophecy was never surrounded by rite or law. There has been of recent years a good deal of talk among scholars about the cultic prophet, about his official status and legal role, but most of this fails to say what is really significant about the "canonical" prophets. Their office was indeed regular, recognized, and official, but it was completely free. Its charisma was not legalized or channeled. It was not assumed, as later it was in the legal Church, that a rite of ordination was effective in the transmission of charisma. Perhaps, then, I may be permitted to say that it is no wonder that large sections of the Church have always looked a bit askance at prophecy, and that the recovery of the prophets has been the work of *Protestant* higher critics.

The prophet was the herald of the divine King, sent to speak a Word not his own. His "Thus saith the Lord" had an authority above all other human authorities. Chosen and empowered by God, no rite of human induction into office was fitting or desirable. His was an office regulated not by the consent of those to whom he was sent, but solely by the divine King. This freedom from human institutionalism was prophecy's greatest strength, though it was also its greatest danger. In the course of time the country was overrun with prophets, most of whom, as Jeremiah put it, got their messages from themselves and the people, rather than from God. Hence Jeremiah hears God's rejection of them: "Behold, I am against the prophets, said the Lord, that steal my words every one from his neighbor" (23:30). So prophecy turned against prophecy, and men like Micaiah, Amos, and Jeremiah dissociated themselves from those whose vocation was increasingly institutionalized and used in support of state and temple, the institutional *status quo*. The freedom permitted by the conception of charisma was greatly abused, even as it is today among the sects, but without that freedom the great prophets would never have arisen, and the Israelite community as a people of God would scarcely have survived the destruction of life, property, and political institutions.

In most natural societies in the past, monarchy and temple, state and religion, were the very foundation and life of the social structure. King and temple were the points of meeting between the eternal and the temporal. Destroy them, and society is destroyed because the security of the superhuman integration is taken away. The natural society, therefore, has its setting in particular world views which tie the structure of the cosmos into the temporal structure of earth. And this tie is customarily made institutionally, through human structures of power and organization. This generalization holds good, I believe, even for such pseudo-religions as Communism. The revolutionary conflict between the "haves" and "have-nots," and the resolution in a classless Utopia, can be believed only because there is posited a rational structure of the cosmos, a universal given which acts that way. Meanwhile, the party institution is the link between the eternal, universal good and the present temporal situation.

In Israel the same attempt was made to secure primary status for king and priest. Yet neither kingship nor temple was able to achieve the absolutism, the sanctity, or the permanence which would make them adequate symbols for the nation's inner life. Israel as a people of God existed before either of them came into being and subsequently continued to exist without them. Israel's golden age was the time of David and Solomon, but the prophets did not appeal to it as a model for community life. Instead, they pointed to the wilderness period when Israel had nothing but a bond between people and Deity which was very close and direct. It was a bond not mediated through the later institutions of state and temple.

It is important to observe that in prophetic eschatology the consummation of the kingdom of God is to be marked by a great revival of charismatic happenings. Both leaders and people will then be Spirit-filled and Spirit-empowered on a scale hitherto unknown, though foreshadowed in the days before the monarchy. A dominant element in scriptural typology is the conception of the end-time as the re-establishment and fulfillment of the beginning, while at the same time it inaugurates a new age. For the prophets the charismatic period of Israel's history was its great and typical age, and the end-time would see its fulfillment: "Not by might, nor by power, but by my Spirit, says the Lord of hosts" (Zech. 4:6, cf. Isa. 11:2, 42:1, 44:3; Ezek. 36:37, 37:14, Joel 2:28 f.).[3]

It is against this background that we comprehend the New Testament's absorption with the work of the Holy Spirit. The new age in Christ is one in which the people of God are led, purified, empowered, and enlightened by the Spirit. For this reason there is in the New Testament no detailed interest in institutionalism of and for itself. It has often been affirmed that the history of the Church during the late first and second centuries of our era is marked by an increasing institutionalism, with its concern for the details of rules and rites and dogma, and with a corresponding diminution of interest in the relation of Church and Holy Spirit. The sub-apostolic thinkers, we are told, actually had no doctrine of the Spirit at all. Yet the primitive Church was almost exclusively a charismatic community. For Paul, as one scholar has written, "the Ecclesia was essentially an almost world-wide fellowship of the Spirit, taking form and name in local congregations, cells in the one Body of the exalted Christ."[4] As was the case in premonarchical Israel and in

[3] The conception of the prophet as a man filled by the Spirit was very common, as may be noted by such revealing passages as Num. 11:26–29; 24:2; I Sam. 10:9–12; 19:20–24; Hos. 9:7; Mic. 2:7 (cf. v. 11); 3:8; Ezek. 2:2; 3:12 etc.; Joel 2:28. It must be noted, however, that the pre-Exilic prophets of the eighth and seventh centuries made little use of the term "Spirit" in relation to their own mission. This may have been because of the large number of popular prophets who so misused the term that it was best avoided; or there may have been other and unknown reasons. In any event, I here use the more comprehensive term "charisma" in relation to the prophetic office in order to broaden the context from a simple concordance investigation to a larger phenomenological perspective.

[4] George Johnson, *The Doctrine of the Church in the New Testament*, p. 111.

later prophecy, leadership was not created by the community. It was given to the Church by the Lord through the work of the Spirit. Word and Spirit had created the community, and the various ministries of the Church were dominantly charismatic. Individuals were understood to have been marked out for this or that special function by the divers gifts (*charismata*) accorded them.

To be sure, the freedom of the Spirit-led community could be abused, even as it was in Israel. The problem of false prophecy and speaking with tongues was very real, so that we read exhortations to "test the spirits whether they are of God" (I John 4:1) and to make sure of the edifying nature of prophecy (I Cor. 14). Yet the Lordship of Christ over the Church was mediated through the Spirit's work, and it was confidently believed that the affirmation of Lordship exercised in this manner was not an ideal or ethereal idea but a most relevant, practical statement. Of course, the work of the Spirit was not in an organizational vacuum. There were developing forms of one sort or another. Affairs were regularized and done in order. Biblical community, however, was conceived primarily as an organism rather than as an organization, and God's direction of community life by Word and Spirit could not be circumscribed by institutions which at best had but a temporal, and usually temporary, function.

III

If this portrayal of the Biblical conception of the rule of God is in any measure correct, then Rudolph Sohm's insight into the meaning of charismatic is confirmed. And the problem thrust at us in our day is a very great one indeed. How does God rule, how can he rule, our vast ecclesiastical organizations? The Church has tried to regulate the charismatic, to control and channel it through law. Yet Christian history has shown this to be impossible, for charisma has a way of breaking out of all bounds, of achieving the unexpected, of violating institutional proprieties. And sober people are often more shocked by the excesses than gratified by the true examples of God's power.

One can argue this question in two directions. On the one hand, it can be said both from experience and from Biblical history that as man is man he cannot live in an ordered society without organizations. And to be ruled by law instead of by anarchy is one of the greatest of all good things. Kingship in Israel became a necessity in order to unify the nation and concentrate its resources against foreign domination. Man cannot worship without some forms of worship, and Israel took over and altered for her purpose certain forms used by all men whom they knew. Any other course was inconceivable. Similarly, it has been said that it was easy enough for the primitive Church to be almost exclusively charismatic when the numbers were small and when the consummation of world history was believed to be at hand. But with growth in numbers and with the unexpected delay in the Second Coming of Christ, something had to be done. I have argued elsewhere that Judaism in post-Exilic times grew up as an answer to the question as to how the people were to live when the great Day of the Lord did not arrive when and as expected. Similarly, it has been argued that the legalization of the Church occurred as an answer to the problem of life within a delayed eschatology. We have to live and we cannot live without meaningful order and form. It is all very well to talk about freedom and the Holy Spirit, but who could live on prophetic one-sided fare alone! And so much of this interest in the charismatic is fostered by those who would separate themselves completely from the historic Church. Is not our sectarianism a vivid example of charismatic freedom becoming ecclesiastical anarchy?

On the other hand, it can be argued that God through the work of the Spirit has always been at war with human institutionalism, because the institution becomes idolatrous, self-perpetuating, and self-worshiping, because Church membership becomes synonymous with the new birth, because man tries to make the Spirit follow law and assume that it is only mediated through rite, etc.

As Rudolph Sohm was among the first in our time to recognize the importance of the charismatic for understanding Church history, so Max Weber was the first to point out its importance as a sociological phenomenon. At every critical juncture of social history, says Weber, there arise "natural" leaders who possess special gifts of body and spirit not accessible to everybody. This charismatic structure is in contrast to any kind of bureaucratic organization of offices. It knows nothing about forms or ordered procedures of appointment and dismissal. "Charisma knows only inner determination and inner restraint. The holder of charisma seizes the task that is adequate for him and demands obedience and a following by virtue of his mission. His success determines whether he finds them. His charismatic claim breaks down if his mission is not recognized by those to whom he feels he has been sent. If they recognize him, he is their master—so long as he knows how to maintain recognition through 'proving' himself. But he does not derive his 'right' from their will, in the manner of an election."[5]

Now every Christian, before he is anything else, is first of all the holder of mysterious gifts, of charisma. He is called and continually empowered by God for a task in this world, a task which is charismatic. The Christian vocation may accommodate itself to certain forms and structures of the world, but it should

[5] *From Max Weber: Essays in Sociology*, tr. by H. H. Gerth and C. W. Mills, 1946, pp. 245 ff.

not and will not be overcome and completely confined by them. The freedom that we have in Christ makes us, as the apostle Paul said, kings who are to make critical judgments. And the resources of the whole fellowship of Christ should be at the disposal of the individual, who is the Church's frontier in the world. The institutional Church, however, is inclined to get this backwards. It sees its task to be that of securing the support of the layman for its program, rather than that of giving all assistance to the layman in his task of being a Christian in his work.

How does God rule our Church? I do not know the answers to all the questions that I have been trying to raise. Rebellious as I am against a tendency toward idolatry in every institution, one surely does not solve the problem simply by starting a new institution for the Spirit! I feel instead that my own calling is within the Church, but it is to be dominated by the charismatic idea, to be so absorbed with God's direct rule, that it becomes a habit of mind continually to interpret meaning and purpose in his activity. If in this absorption I am loyal to the Church, and yet not as blindly idolatrous of its institutional features as are some of my friends, then I cannot help it. If this absorption leads me at times to attempt the role of critical prophet so that I am not an entirely safe man for the ecclesiastical hierarchy, then I cannot help that either. Precisely how God rules through the bureaucratic structure and promotional programs of the Church, I do not know. But I do not believe he is defeated even there. My first business is with my calling in and through the Church; that is my salvation to be fulfilled with fear and trembling. And I do not believe that the episcopacy as a form of Church government, or the Presbyterian or Congregational systems, mean as much to God as they do to certain of his earthly representatives!

7

THE GIFTS OF GOD:
THE BIBLICAL VIRTUES

The most familiar text which we might use for discussion of our topic is I Corinthians 13:13: "And now abideth faith, hope and love, these three, and the greatest of these is love."

Or we might use Ephesians 3:14–21, where we note certain key phrases: "that Christ may dwell in your hearts *through faith*," that you "being rooted and *grounded in love*," that you may *"comprehend," "know," "be filled."* These verses present God's spiritual gifts: faith, love, and a comprehension of all things that may lead one to wait, to hope, to stand firm.

Or we might turn to the last verses of Psalm 31 in the Old Testament:

> *O Love the Lord, all his loyal ones;*
> *The faithful the Lord protects,*

But requiteth in abundance the haughty doer.
Be strong, and let your heart take courage,
All you who wait for the Lord.

Let us pause for a few moments on this Psalm. Like so many of the meditations and prayers of the Old Testament it was written by a man in deep distress, a distress such as few of us are forced to encounter.

What the trouble is we do not know.

V. 4.	He says he is in a net set to trap him.
V. 9.	His whole being is wasted with grief; his strength is gone.
Vv. 11–13, 15, 18, 20.	He is scorned by enemies, an object of dread to his friends, avoided in the streets. He thinks there is terror, scheming, and plotting against him, all around. He is surrounded with the contempt, the lies, the strife of tongues, of the proud and insolent.
V. 21.	Thus he feels as though he were shut in a besieged city.
V. 12.	He is like a broken vessel, or a dead man; he is deprived of everything in life but fear and suffering.

In other words, here is a man crying out of the depths, outraged and broken by the injustices of society, helpless, abandoned, alone and lonely, with absolutely nothing left to hope for or to believe in as far as society is concerned.

So many of the Psalmists picture some similar situation—sickness, death, disgrace, or danger have so enveloped them that there is nothing left in themselves or in society to give them hope or confidence. They often describe their plight as sinking deep within the waters of the primeval ocean. Nothing is left for them.

Yet their confidence in God and their triumphant expressions of trust and hope in God mount in reverse proportion to the seriousness of their plight. In pouring out their woe before God they alternate their urgent requests for aid with the most confident affirmation of faith.

Our Psalmist speaks repeatedly of God as his stronghold, his rock and fortress. He prays that God be a rock of refuge for him, and then states:

> *for thou art my refuge.*
> *Into thy hand I commit my spirit.*
> *Thou hast redeemed me, O Faithful God.*

Now he scarcely possesses a sufficient vocabulary to express the greatness of God's love, his faithfulness and justice. He turns from his own story, and addresses the whole community. "Let every one of God's faithful people, everyone who waits in hope and trust, let him take heart, let him love the Lord who is the faithful God."

The depth of the Psalmist's horror has been invaded by the glory of the wondrous God. And this has produced the most marvelous expression of faith, love, and hope: faith in the faithful God; love for the God who has acted in such a loving way; hope in the God who has here and always shown himself the refuge of the needy.

Would to God that I, that each one of us, had such an unshakable and joyous confidence in God, that we could speak with such assurance and conviction of our love for him! Faith, love, hope—these summarize the whole range of Christian virtues (as we know from the way they are so often used together in the Bible, and especially in the New Testament). How on earth can I acquire them? By what means can I lay hold on the Psalmist's faith?

I

As far as I know, the Bible nowhere tells us precisely how we can lay hold. Instead, we are simply exhorted over and over again to have faith and be faithful, to love and to hope.

Note, for example, the following phrases: "if ye have faith, and doubt not," "how is it ye have no faith," "have faith in God," "where is your faith," "continue in the faith," "hast thou faith," "increase our faith," etc. We are never given a formula, a discipline, a set of rules or procedures, a series of devotional readings and exercises, which are guaranteed or even supposed to produce faith, hope, and love in us. We are simply exhorted. This seems strange. If these things are so important, there ought to be something we can *do* to get them.

One of the key doctrines of modern education is that the virtues can be taught, that we can be trained in morals, that goodness is a habit which can be gained through knowledge and practice, that it is a human achievement. Our aim is no longer simply to teach the three R's, how to read, write, and number, but it has become character education, the education of the whole man for integrated life so that he be a good citizen. The value of religion is that it is a fine aid in building character by stressing the fatherhood of God and the brotherhood of man. Our religious education movement has been rooted in these conceptions. Today we are beginning to see that we need more theology in religious teaching, but that is only because we have become uncertain as to just how far we can go with character education. Nevertheless, the pragmatic value of theology to produce good character is still a central concern—even, it seems to me, in a good deal of the material for teachers and parents in our Church School materials.

Medieval and Catholic theology to a certain extent have assisted this point of view. This theology agrees with Plato and Aristotle that the cardinal virtues are *prudence, fortitude* or *bravery, temperance,* and *justice*. But these are the natural virtues, possessed by all men. To them are to be added, like the frosting on a cake, the theological virtues of faith, hope, and love which come from God by revelation.

Now I am not sure, at all, just what our Psalmist would have said to all this. Certainly he would not have said that faith is something which God adds to his natural bravery, or that love is God's addition to a goodness he is able to achieve by habit. But he certainly would agree that faith, hope, and love are from God, and not from himself, that they are gifts and not his achievements.

It is true that to a certain extent virtue as habit can be taught, that decency can be communicated from generation to generation. Yet the Church's effort in character education has discovered that we cannot produce faith, hope, and love by teaching alone. So today we are giving great attention to devotions and devotional literature and Bible reading. Surely, the Christian virtues can be formed in this way.

Yet here, for example, are two faithful, hard-working, and devotionally minded Church people, and both are regular users of devotional literature. Tragedy strikes the homes of both. One collapses completely; he possesses no reserve of strength; there is no glory to relieve the stark tragedy, no faith to penetrate the gloom. Entrance into and ministry to such a home is as difficult as it is challenging. The other, while suffering no less keenly, radiates with a hope and faith that have driven tragedy from the door. There is no self-pity, no sorrow for the state of the loved one lost; there is only a heart and soul outstretched to God, accepting, trusting, confident even in weakness: "Though he slay me, yet will I trust him!"

In other words, faith, hope, and love are not virtues which we can compel, or achieve as habits, or teach to others. They are the mysterious gifts of God to his faithful. We cannot force them into ourselves; they are not our achievements. They have to do with gifts and response to gifts.

And they are not states of character, but they are given or instilled in us as relations to others and especially to God. Love is formed in me as a gift from the object of love. The Psalmist exhorts us to love God because God has acted in such a way as to instill love in us. We have faith in the form of complete trust because God has shown himself to be the Faithful One. We trust him because he attracts trust, forms it in us. We hope because he has given us hope. It is thus clear that to the Biblical man the great virtues are responses, not habits. They are gifts of God, not something we ourselves can achieve and make into states of character. No wonder, then, that the Bible does not give us a set of rules so that we can get them.

Furthermore, as Professor H. Richard Niebuhr has pointed out, they can scarcely be said to be *additions* to natural virtues we all possess. They rather reform and restore the love, faith, and hope which God has placed in us and in our relations with others. We all have love in us, but we often give it to idols. We have faith and trust, but in a world of unworthy objects our trust becomes mixed with mistrust, our loyalty to partial causes betrays other causes. Hence love and hate, trust and mistrust, faith and infidelity become involved in one another. In a world of broken promises, and in a past full of betrayal and disappointment, hope turns into hopelessness (or into Utopianism mixed with anxiety). Faith, hope, and love as gifts from God do not add something not already present; they reform, they restore, they heal our perverted capacities for hopeful, loving, and faithful response to God and to others.

118

The Gifts of God

It is important to recall that the attributes of God in the Bible are nearly all words depicting relationship between persons. Israel's greatest liturgical confession, based on such attributes, is found in Exodus 34:6–7. There the old confession is placed in the mouth of God himself as he reveals himself to Moses. A great tenth-century theological historian (the Yahwist writer) has used it to summarize the whole of God's self-revelation in history, and the attributes mentioned describe his nature as he has made it known in his acts toward Israel:

> *God is compassionate and gracious, slow to anger [i.e. patient], full of lovingkindness and truth [that is, faithfulness in keeping promises]; keeping lovingkindness for thousands, forgiving iniquity, transgression and sin; but he will by no means acquit the guilty; instead he is one who visits the iniquities of the fathers upon the children, and the children's children unto the third, even the fourth generation.*

As God is gracious, patient, full of lovingkindness, faithful and righteous in all his ways, so man is to exhibit the same qualities in his relationship to his fellowmen. This is man's service; it is his love and devotion to God. Social obligation becomes obedient response to the gracious God. The attributes of God become the attributes of the man of faith.

The reason for this lies in the relationship which God has created between himself and his people. To depict it, one may recall the various relationships which bind us to one another. Most of them involve ties of blood or family, bonds created by various legal relationships, vocational associations, and the like. Yet there is one special type of bond that we easily forget. Here, for example, is a great-hearted person, usually one older or superior to me in some way, who for some mysterious reason, known only to himself, does a gracious, loving deed, or shows a special favor to me. Each of us is what he is today in no small measure because of such gracious gifts of love, friendship, assistance which we did not deserve and had no right to expect. In most instances there can be no question of repayment. We can only learn the art of humble, grateful acceptance. Yet such an act of love pulls me to the giver of love. A bond is created, and I am led to respond in love. The gift of the giver implants a loving response in me. Love then is both a gift and a response. And to betray the bond thus created is instinctly felt to be the most heartless, faithless, and scandalous of personal actions. Indeed, betrayal of this type of relationship would appear to be one of the primary sources of both conscious and subconscious feelings of guilt.

The relationship between God and people in the Bible is of this type. Before it is described in language drawn from the family, from law, or from international treaties, it is a relationship created by the gracious action of God. In the great confession quoted above, one of the central words is the Hebrew *hesed*, translated "lovingkindness," or "mercy," or "steadfast love." The truth of the matter is that the word is really untranslatable, for it refers to the gifts and responses made in the bond established by grace. *Hesed* is what God has done to us, to tie us to himself in a gracious relationship. And *hesed* is what we owe him in return—what he both implants in us as a gift and pulls from us as a response.[1]

It is in this light that we are to understand God's attributes as descriptive of those divine actions which define his relationship to us. And the Christian virtues are the responses, the *hesed*, which he both gives and draws from us. They are terms of re-

---

[1] These remarks are derived from a fresh (but unpublished) study of this Hebrew word by Professor Sidney Hills of Western Theological Seminary in Pittsburgh.

lationship; they exist only in relationship; and it is small wonder, then, that they cannot be taught to people who know nothing of the relationship which alone brings them into being.

II

Now another thing about the great Christian virtues, as Professor Niebuhr has further pointed out, is that we Christians are always trying to simplify them and to assume that one of them is the sum of all the rest. Thus in preparation for the Evanston Assembly of the World Council of Churches hope was dominant in theological discussion. If we have hope, then presumably we have what is important. This is a hopeless world; and if we can give it hope, then presumably we Christians have done our work well. Hence in the first two reports of the Advisory Committee of the World Council, put out in 1951 and 1952, there was scarcely any mention of faith and love. Hope, evidently, crowded out the others or was dealt with apart from the others as though it were the sum of the Christian religion. This was perhaps not intentional, but it occurred.

Then again the Reformation placed all emphasis upon faith. "The just shall live by faith"; faith saves, not works of love and goodness. Faith is God's gift, and our response of faith is accepted for righteousness. So in Protestant orthodoxy faith is central, but as that orthodoxy survives today *faith as belief* is all that is necessary. A *secondary form of faith, namely belief*, is what God requires for salvation. Yet faith as belief in a series of propositions can and does exist without love and completely without social compassion. Which is worse, a loveless believer or a loveless pagan? I am not sure. They have certain characteristics in common. Understanding this, we can agree with the Epistle of James that "faith without works is dead," and we can agree with Paul that the greatest of the three is love.

So in modern Protestantism, by and large, the main emphasis has been characteristically placed upon love. If we love, what need do we have of anything else? We will have everything else. But the trouble with love is that it can become a weak sentimentality and it can exist without faith and hope. Hosea loved the harlot Gomer, but he surely had no faith in her. A fine woman can love a gangster even when she has no faith in him. Love without faith, or without trust and loyalty, can be lacking in morality completely. The Church can proclaim love when it has no faith. Only when love is combined with faith does it become great love. True love may be the greatest of the virtues, but it cannot exist without faith and hope.

In other words, these three virtues are all bound up in one another, but they are not identical with one another. There is a unity in the Christian life which no separation of virtues can describe. And to distinguish faith, hope, and love is not to split this unity. These words simply describe various aspects of it.

Love exists as the movement of our being toward One whose graciousness both instills and invites it. It refers to the most intimate and close of all emotional attachments, and it always presupposes a subject and an object.

But what is faith? To us it is primarily *belief* in something we cannot prove. In the Bible, however, the words for faith presuppose an utter and complete *commitment*, in which there are two main elements: trust and faithfulness, complete reliance and entire loyalty. *Belief in* the object of faith is presupposed, but faith as belief does not receive the major emphasis. Instead, it is faith as trust and as fidelity to the Faithful One.

Recall the Biblical Abraham, the story of whom was used by Paul in the New Testament to prove that faith is primary and takes precedence over obedience to legal forms. The tradition about him does not give us a connected story, but only various episodes, each preserved originally perhaps for a different reason. But the first collector of these traditions in writing saw in them one central theme, which he summarized in the verse: Abraham "believed in the Lord; and he reckoned it to him for righteousness" (Gen. 15:6). That is, it was the Patriarch's belief, or faith, that was the occasion for his acceptance by God. And what was the nature of this belief?

The Genesis stories about the Patriarchs are, as a whole, given meaning by the election promises of God, repeated to each Patriarch. Subsequent events, then, namely, the Exodus, the Conquest, the reign of David, become fulfillments of these promises. In no case is God's choice of, or promises to, a Patriarch determined by any superior righteousness or goodness of character on the part of the recipient. Any moralistic attempt to prove Isaac better than Ishmael, or Jacob better than Esau, is doomed to failure. God's motives are hidden in his mysterious grace; he chooses whom he will, taking men as they are and making even their sin to serve him.

Now Abraham is the recipient of these wonderful promises. They are three in number: (1) a great nation shall arise from his loins; (2) that "in thee and thy seed all the families of the earth shall bless themselves" (Gen. 12:2–3); and (3) "Unto thy seed will I give this land" (v. 7).

Yet these very promises furnish a spiritual problem. No sooner is the Patriarchal family in Palestine than they are troubled with a famine, and have to go to Egypt. Fearing for his safety because of his beautiful wife, Abraham is caught in Egypt lying about her and saying she is his sister (Gen. 12:10–20). This action causes such trouble that God has to intervene in order to straighten things out. Then again, the promises are wonderful, but a son is needed if they are to be fulfilled. How can two old people have a son? Sarah cannot believe it, but thinks she had better help matters along according to the practical wisdom contained in a custom of the day. She gave her slave, Hagar, to Abraham, that she might be "built" from her. Yet this promptly involved the family in a squabble (Gen. 16), as is the case with practically every polygamous Old Testament family. Again God has to step in and solve the problem. This is the context of the famous verse: Abraham "believed in the Lord." That is, he trusted God; he believed God would do what he promised. Abraham needed only to trust and to wait in patience.

Faith here is represented very simply as commitment and trust, a type of belief which is centered, not primarily in law or in a principle, but in a Faithful Person. It is a commitment and a trust so firmly rooted in that Person as to govern action and lead to obedience. Conversely, sin is born of doubt and nourished by anxiety. In new and problematical situations faith as trust becomes difficult, but lack of trust leads to faithless actions which plunge a man ever deeper into trouble. This is the perennial problem of even the good man, who wants to believe, yet in his anxiety cannot *wait* upon God. Faith like love always involves a relationship, not a state of character. It presupposes a freedom on our part to attach ourselves, to bind ourselves to an object of faith, and also a freedom either to keep or to break our promises and covenants. Thus faith as trust presupposes an object which has instilled trust in us. And faith as faithfulness involves a moral response on our part. Hence the great Biblical text: "The just shall live by faith" (Heb. 2:4) means that we are to live in complete fidelity to God and to our promises to God, because God has shown himself to be trusted; he is the Faithful One.

Hope, on the other hand, presupposes *time*—a past, a present, and a future. We hope because we know the Faithful One will redeem our past and present, and give us a nobler future. Faith and love are not necessarily characterized by this time reference, though hope apart from faith and love is empty and vain.

In other words, each of the great Biblical virtues has its own distinctive character: love is an intimate attachment to the gracious and lovely One. Faith is trust in and faithfulness to our covenant with the Faithful One, a trust that annihilates fear and a faithfulness that involves our neighbor. And there is hope in the action of the Faithful One to provide a future, undeserved, and yet one for which we can wait with confidence.

In the Bible it is thus clear that no one of these virtues can be seen in action without the others. In the words of our Psalmist:

Love the Lord, all his faithful ones (for God is he who has always acted in love, and is always faithful). Therefore be of good courage, all who wait in hope and trust.

III

So far so good! But we are back where we started. How do we obtain these great virtues for which all of us long so deeply? If they are gifts of God and always involve responses to God, it would seem that I cannot obtain them by myself. If I have them, fine! If not, too bad! What can I do—nothing?

It would certainly appear that if, as with happiness, I start chasing after them, and exercise no end of physical and spiritual skill in the chase, I will never catch up with them. They will always elude me.

I must seek something else, or rather I must seek the One who gives, and then trust that in this search these gifts will arrive in such measure as he wills. They are his rewards. I cannot claim

125

them as my right; I cannot seize them from him. I can only seek God himself, and continue my search for him as long as I live.

But how can I do that? I am told: "Seek ye the Lord that he may be found"—but how can I find him?

Well, first of all, there is Jesus Christ. The more we study him the more real God becomes. There is something in that study which leads us to God. The Holy Spirit is at work here and by some mysterious alchemy the knowledge of God is formed. Yet, nevertheless, Christ may seem many centuries removed from our day. The living Christ can elude us even when we search for him. To have the idea is not completely to possess it. The importance of the Bible, as it is summarized and given point and unity in Christ, is, however, that in it the true God stands revealed as our Lord—the Lord who demands that we serve him and who has redeemed us that we may serve him.

This confronts us, as it did Biblical man, with a decision. Can I accept God's redeeming acts, can I accept his forgiveness as a free gift, and then answer his call to service? Can I undertake *his* marching orders, concentrate my attention on *him* as my Commander, and on no one else? Can I enter his gracious covenant, join the society of forgiven sinners which he has formed, and of which Christ is the Head, and through that society pursue with single-minded devotion the calling, the vocation given me?

Jesus said: "Not everyone that says 'Lord, Lord' shall enter the Kingdom of heaven, but he that *doeth the will* of my Father."

So the first thing I can *do* is to seek my calling, and then do it with all the loyalty and fidelity I can muster. And for that *now* is the important time, not tomorrow or five years from now, when I may be doing something that I like better. To lose myself now in the tasks, even in the drudgery, of God's calling, that is to find myself.

And yet this is not enough in itself. To do my duty even though it kills me may be and is a fine thing, but there may be no glory or joy in it—the glory and joy that come from outside me. There must be a continuous effort of will to understand and to interpret what God is doing. God stands revealed to us in Scripture as the active, the living God, the Lord of earth, the Lord of the Church, and the Lord of my life. The final proof and the certainty of God can never come from all our arguments about him, or from all our need of him to explain how the world was started. Certainty comes from the interpretation of life and history. It comes from a daring, intellectual feat: the courage to say that what has happened in Scripture, in history, and in my life is not accidental or self-explanatory—it is the activity of God.

The whole of our Psalmist's case and his exhortation to love, trust, and hope is based upon his argument from his people's history and from his own experience. He knows! There is no use in arguing his interpretation. God is the Faithful One, the Loving One, and the One for whom we can expectantly wait. Sin, tragedy, frustration only confirm his certainty. His people have been saved and led by God, and he himself has been redeemed from his darkness. His certainty has come from his interpretation of the acts of God, the living, ever-present God, the God who is encountered constantly—not simply or solely in private inner experience, but in daily life with all its mixture of horror and hope, of tragedy and salvation.

It is this constant, expectant seeking of God in the midst of our vocation, the interpretation of the past as we walk in the present toward the future—this is life *with* God and *under* God. This is *seeking* him while he may be found, calling upon him while he is near. And unless we say that the Bible is wrong, we must also assume that it is in this search that God accords us faith, hope, and love, gifts which he places within us, which become our responses to him, and which reform our love, our faith, and our hope in one another.

This, then, is the source of the Psalmist's confidence in the faithful, loving God, the confidence which enables him to exhort his people:

> *Love the Lord, all his loyal ones . . .*
> *Be strong and let your heart take courage,*
>   *All you who wait for the Lord.*

INDEX

as personal, 11, 12, 18, 42; as Presence, 72; as Ruler, 50, 52, 100, 101 f.; as Shepherd, 50; as Spirit, 4, 11; as stronghold (rock), 115; as the Known, 53; as the One, 127; as the Unknown, 11; as transcendent, 16; as Will, 53

God, activity of, 127; attributes of, 119; doctrine of, 17; experience of, 49; fear of, 54; goodness of, 29, 31, 62, 99, 119 f.; "image of," 30; in Christ, 47; Kingdom of, 43, 52; knowledge of, 49, 51, 53 ff.; love of, 91, 115; purpose of, 54; vengeance of, 32

God's: blessing, 55; "dwelling," 71; gifts, 113 ff.; grace, 42, 44, 53; house. *See* "House of God"; name, 70 f.; presence, 71, 72, 84, 85, 89; promises, 82, 85, 123 f.; redemptive purpose, 45; rule, 100 ff.; self-revelation, 119

Gods, 8, 17, 62 ff., 86, 88

Gospel, 89, 92

Government, 100 ff.

Guilt, 120

Harnack, 98, 99

Haroutunian, Joseph, 90

Heaven, 11

Hell, 11

Hesed, 120

Hexateuch, 24

Hinduism, 49 f.

Historical: memory, 69, 74; revelation, 13

History, 11, 26, 126 f.

Holiness, 12

Holy Spirit, 4, 95 ff., 105, 126

Hope, 106 ff.

"House of God," 59 ff., 79 ff.

House of Prayer, 71

Humanism, 44

Idealism, 13

Idolatry, 48

Immortality, 12

Incarnation, 4

Individual, responsibility of, 42, 43, 54, 86 ff.

Individualism, 39, 40, 41, 43, 44, 45, 54 ff.

Infinity, 10

Institutionalism, 102 ff.

Isaiah, 32, 48 f., 83 f.

Isaiah (Second), 5 ff., 11, 16 f.

Jacob, 60

Jacob, Philip E., 90, 91

Jehoiakim, 81, 82

Jeremiah, 41, 49, 79 ff., 103

Jerusalem: priesthood, 24 f., 71–73; temple, 61, 69 ff., 82

Jesus Christ. *See* Christ

Jews, 73

Job, 84, 86, 90

Josiah. *See* Reform

Judah, 5, 71, 81 ff.

Judaism, 23, 51, 101

Judgment, 7, 31, 32, 87

Judges, Book of, 100

Justice, 18, 54, 86 ff., 115

Kierkegaard, S., 13

King, 103 f.

Kingdom of God, 104

Kingship, 100 ff., 107

Knowledge, 52, 53, 116; communication of, 50; tree of. *See* Tree

Knowledge of God. *See* God

Lamech, 32

Law, 42 f., 47, 50 f., 73, 84, 97 ff., 107; ecclesiastical, 97 ff.

Index

Leadership, human, 99 ff., 104, 108
Life, apart from God, 32; interpretation of, 25 ff., 127; renewal of, 69
Lord's Supper, 75 f.
Lordship of Christ, 106
Love, 106 ff.; brotherly, 12, 54; for Christ, 52; for God, 86; of my neighbor, 47, 86
Lovingkindness. See *Hesed*

Magic, 68, 89
Man, 12, 26 ff., 30, 33, 38, 39, 43, 45, 50, 62, 86, 97, 107, 116, 118, 124, 126; doctrine of, 30; of faith, 119; of God, 55; humanistic view of, 39, 44; and society, 39 ff., 44 ff., 54, 86
Mass, the, 73, 74
Mendenhall, George E., 50, 51
Mercy. See *Hesed*
Mesopotamia, 62 f.
Messiah, 75
Mythology, 11, 27, 62, 64 f. See also Gilgamish

New society. See Society
New Testament, 43, 46, 48, 51 f., 72, 73, 89, 97, 98, 100, 105, 115
Niebuhr, H. Richard, 33 f., 118, 121
Numbers, Book of, 24

Obedience, 12, 42 f., 53, 55, 79 ff.
Old Testament, understanding of community, 41 ff., 86 ff., 100 ff., 106 ff.
Ontology, 14 ff.
Ordination, 102

Parables, 25
Paradise, 23 ff.
Passover, 68 f., 75
Paton, Alan, 39

Patriarchs, 122 f.
Paul, the Apostle, 19, 49, 105, 109, 122
Peace, 88 ff.
"People of God," 41 ff., 54, 68 ff., 97 ff., 104 f., 119 f.
Polytheism, 18, 61 ff.
Prayer, 12, 70, 84; of Solomon, 70
Priestly program, 83 ff.
Priests, 82 ff., 102. *See also* Jerusalem priesthood
Prophecy, 103
Prophets, 74 ff., 100 ff., 109; false, 48, 82 ff., 103, 106
Protestant: principle, 17; orthodoxy, 121
Protestantism, Protestants, 11, 74, 103, 121 f.

Reality, 53
Redemption, 5, 12, 45
Reform (of Josiah), 81, 82
Reformation, 121
Religion, 17, 91, 116
Religiosity, 84
Religious teaching, 116
Response to God, 119 f., 124 f., 128
Revelation, 13, 19, 44, 69, 101
Rite, 67, 68, 69, 73 f., 75, 98 f., 102
Ritual, 67 f., 69
Romig, Theodore F., 37, 39
Rule of God. See God

Sacraments, 45, 67, 68 ff., 74, 75, 99
Sacrifices and offerings, 64 f., 68, 74
Salvation, 69, 75 f., 109, 121
Sectarianism, 40, 107
Security, 84, 88 f., 91
Sermon on the Mount, 43
Sin, 26, 31, 32, 33, 47, 85, 127; original, 33
Sinners, 52, 91
Social justice, 86 ff.

Index

Society, 96, 103, 114; biblical doctrine of, 50, 86 f., 101; breakdown of, 39; Christian, 40; "the New," 43, 45, 50, 97; organization of, 12, 45, 101, 103, 106

Sohm, Rudolph, 97, 99, 106, 108

Solomonic Temple, 69, 70

Spirit, 11, 12, 19, 48, 96, 104, 105, 106, 108; of Christ, 98; of God, 98, 101. *See also* God; Holy Spirit

Spiritual: essence (soul), 11, 12
experience, 12
gifts. *See* Gifts; need, 95 f.

Stuart, J. L. 38

Student, Typical American, 90 f.

Symbols, 18 f., 26, 65 f., 69 ff., 98

Synagogue, 71, 73

Tabernacle, 69, 71, 72, 74

Temple, 83, 88, 103 f., as "house of God." *See* House; as house of prayer, 70, 71, 74; of Bethel, 61; of Jerusalem. *See* Jerusalem; pagan, 61 f., 65; theology, 70 ff.

"Temple of the Lord," 79, 82, 83

Theology. *See* Biblical; Catholic

Tillich, Paul, 4, 14–19

Tolerance, limit of., 48

Totalitarianism, 34, 38 f.

Transcendence, (of God), 10, 16, 70

Transubstantiation, 73 f.

Tree, of life, 26, 28 ff.; of knowledge, 29, 29 f.

Trust, 122, 124, 125

Truth, 99

Universalism, 45

Universe. *See also* Cosmology of Bible

Utopia, Utopianism, 10, 50, 104, 118

Virtues, 116, 117 ff. *See also* Christian virtues

Vocation, 9, 12, 31, 43, 45, 48 f., 52, 55, 56, 75, 108, 126, 127

Weber, Max, 108

Will, free, 30; human, 30, 32, 47, 68, 69; of God, 30, 69

Word, the, 43, 86, 103, 106

Worship, 45, 47, 55, 68 f., 72, 86–88, 107

Worshiper, pagan, 63, 68

Yahweh, 8

Yahwist (document, writer), 24 ff., 31, 33, 119

Ziggurat, 66, 70